The Survival Guide For Kids With Behavior Challenges

How To Make Good Choices And Stay Out Of Trouble

Thomas McIntyre. Ph.D.
Edited By Marjorie Lisovskis

EasyRead Large

Copyright Page from the Original Book

Text copyright © 2013, 2003 by Tom McIntyre, Ph.D.
Illustrations copyright © 2013, 2003 by Free Spirit Publishing Inc.

All rights reserved under International and Pan-American Copyright Conventions. Unless otherwise noted, no part of this book may be reproduced, stored in a retrieval system, or transmitted in any form or by any means, electronic, mechanical, photocopying, recording or otherwise, without express written permission of the publisher, except for brief quotations or critical reviews. For more information, go to www.freespirit.com/company/permissions.cfm.

Free Spirit, Free Spirit Publishing, and associated logos are trademarks and/or registered trademarks of Free Spirit Publishing Inc. A complete listing of our logos and trademarks is available at www.freespirit.com.

Library of Congress Cataloging-in-Publication Data
McIntyre, Thomas, 1952-
 [Behavior survival guide for kids]
 The survival guide for kids with behavior challenges : how to make good choices and stay out of trouble / Thomas McIntyre. — Revised & updated edition.
   pages cm
 Revised edition of the author's The behavior survival guide for kids : how to make good choices and stay out of trouble, published in 2003.
 Summary: "Many kids and teens have challenges when it comes to behavior. In this revised edition of his time-tested book, Thomas McIntyre provides up-to-date information, practical strategies, and sound advice to help kids learn to make smarter choices, make and keep friends, get along with teachers, take responsibility for their actions, work toward positive change, and enjoy the results of their better behavior. New to this edition are an "Are you ready to change?" quiz, updated glossary and resources, and a fresh organization and design. This is a book for any young person who needs help with behavior. A special section at the back addresses diagnosed behavior disorders." — Provided by publisher.
 Audience: Age 9 to 14.
 ISBN-13: 978-1-57542-449-1 (pbk.)
 ISBN-10: 1-57542-449-5 (pbk.)
 1. Problem children—Juvenile literature. 2. Behavior modification—Juvenile literature. I. Title.
 HQ773.M35 2013
 649'.64—dc23
                                                    2013019727

eBook ISBN: 978-1-57542-633-4

Free Spirit Publishing does not have control over or assume responsibility for author or third-party websites and their content. At the time of this book's publication, all facts and figures cited within are the most current available. All telephone numbers, addresses, and website URLs are accurate and active; all publications, organizations, websites, and other resources exist as described in this book; and all have been verified as of May 2013. If you find an error or believe that a resource listed here is not as described, please contact Free Spirit Publishing. Parents, teachers, and other adults: We strongly urge you to monitor children's use of the Internet.

For privacy reasons, the names of the kids and teachers who are quoted in this book and included in its stories have been changed.

The study referenced in "It's Tough to Be a Kid with BD" (pages 134–135) was conducted by B. Behre, T. McIntyre, and K. Rogers (1993) and is reported in "They Tell Me I'm Crazy: Student Responses to Being Labeled Behavior Disordered." *Perceptions*, 27(4), 12–13.

"Adults You Might Talk To" (page 26) is adapted from "Adults Who Can Help" in *How to Take the Grrrr Out of Anger* by Elizabeth Verdick and Marjorie Lisovskis (Minneapolis: Free Spirit Publishing, 2002), pp. 24–25. Used with permission.

Reading Level Grade 5; Interest Level Ages 9–14;
Fountas & Pinnell Guided Reading Level V

Cover and interior book design: Michelle Lee Lagerroos
Cover illustrations: Steven Hauge
Assistant editors: Douglas Fehlen and Alison Behnke
Illustrations: Chris Sharp
Shark Random Funnyness font: Aryel Filipe

10 9 8 7 6 5 4 3 2
Printed in the United States of America
S18861113

Free Spirit Publishing Inc.
Minneapolis, MN
(612) 338-2068
help4kids@freespirit.com
www.freespirit.com

Free Spirit offers competitive pricing.
Contact edsales@freespirit.com for pricing information on multiple quantity purchases.

TABLE OF CONTENTS

Praise for the previous edition:	i
INTRODUCTION: How This Book Can Help You	ix
The Six Great Gripes of Kids with Behavior Challenges	xix
CHAPTER 1: Are You Ready?	1
CHAPTER 2: Four Smart Choices for Dealing with Feelings	12
CHAPTER 3: Another Smart Choice for Dealing with Feelings	45
CHAPTER 4: Three Survival Skills for Dealing with Difficult People	68
CHAPTER 5: Ways to Help Yourself Make Good Choices in School	88
CHAPTER 6: Ways to Get Along Better with Teachers	115
CHAPTER 7: Ways to Make and Keep Friends	141
CHAPTER 8: Ways to Help the Adults at Home Help YOU	161
CHAPTER 9: More Ideas for Feeling Good at Home	186
CHAPTER 10: Six Winning Ways to Work Toward Positive Change	204
SPECIAL SECTION: What If You Have Been Given a BD Label?	225
CHAPTER 11: What Is BD?	228
CHAPTER 12: Different Kids, Different Causes for BD	240
CHAPTER 13: Why Am I in a Program for Kids with BD?	256
And Now...	279
Glossary	282
Solutions to Some of the Challenges and Questions	296

Resources for You	304
What About Resources for Grown-Ups?	312
Back Cover Material	314
Index	317

Praise for the previous edition:

"A sensitive and thorough title for all collections."
—*School Library Journal*

"Excellent material."
—*Voice of Youth Advocates*

"Kids who use this book will not only make their own lives better, but also ease the lives of family adults, classmates, and teachers."
—*Steven R. Forness, Ph.D., Distinguished Professor Emeritus of Psychiatry and Biobehavioral Sciences at UCLA*

"A great book—very practical and helpful.
Positive, encouraging, and supportive."
—*Eleanor Guetzloe, Professor Emerita, Department of Special Education, University of South Florida*

"Encouraging ... Parents of children with behavior challenges would benefit from reading this book."
—*Children's Literature*

Dedication

While writing this book, I thought a lot about the students I used to teach. They were all working hard to beat behavior challenges. Many of the things that we ask you to try in this book are things that helped them make their lives better in school and at home. We learned together, so I want to dedicate this book to them.

I also want to dedicate this book to my first family. As I was growing up, they always supported me in my efforts to improve my life. My wife and two children have joined them in making my life fun and rewarding.

Thank You

Even though my name is on the front of this book, it's important to let you know that I was part of a team. Many people helped me write the book. I would like to thank them:

Thanks to Ms. Dorota Koczewska and her students who have behavior disorders. (A behavior disorder means that a kid has been making many poor behavior choices, and must work very hard with the teacher to learn to make better choices.) Many of the things said by boys and girls in this book are from kids in Ms. Koczewska's class.

Other teachers like Ms. Kirstin Larson and Mr. John Schmidt read the book before it was finished. They told me ways to change the book to make it even better. Dr. Beth Russell, a principal, also reviewed the book and gave me good ideas. So did Ms. Denise Poston, a researcher and parent of a kid who has been working on making good choices. Another helper was Ms. Debra Carlson, who works with parents of kids who have behavior disorders.

The people I worked with the most were Margie Lisovskis and Alison Behnke, the editors of this book. These hardworking women helped me write things better so that you could understand them better. They also gave me some great ideas to use in the book. Other people at Free Spirit Publishing worked to make this book a good one, too. Judy Galbraith, Free Spirit's president, came up with the idea for the book and asked me to write it.

Douglas Fehlen found lots of information that I needed and worked with Ms. Lisovskis to help me write a better book. Michelle Lee Lagerroos was the designer of this updated edition of the book. An artist named Chris Sharp drew the cartoons.

Now I want to thank **YOU** for reading the book! Winning at your behavior challenge isn't easy. It will require you to think differently in many situations that you face. There will be times when you'll make mistakes. But if you are making more good choices than before, you can be proud of your progress. That progress tells you that you're on the right path. Keep believing in yourself and your ability to meet your goals. Good luck to you as you work hard to make your life better. Oh—wait! It's not luck that is important. It's the other part of that sentence: hard work (and believing in yourself and your ability to make good choices).

Meet Dr. Mac

Hi! I'm Tom McIntyre (Mack-in-tire). I used to be a teacher of kids who had "behavior challenges." These students were working hard to change their behavior. Now I'm a professor at a college. I teach teachers how to work better with kids who need extra help learning more quickly and behaving better. Teachers and kids call me "Dr. Mac." I have two websites for parents and teachers who want to help kids make better behavior choices, stay out of trouble, and enjoy life more. These sites are ParentingDoneRight.info and BehaviorAdvisor.com.

When I have free time and am looking for excitement, I paddle my kayak on river rapids or play handball against a wall. When I want peace and quiet, I take a walk in the woods or go to the public library to read a good book.

Dr. Mac

INTRODUCTION

How This Book Can Help You

- Is it hard for you to follow the rules in school and at home? Do you wish you were better at following the rules and getting along with others?
- Would you like to get in trouble less often?
- Do you have a hard time sitting still or staying in one place?
- Is it sometimes hard for you to concentrate on learning because you keep thinking about your feelings, or

about problems that happened earlier?
- Have you hit people or yelled at them when you've gotten angry or upset? Would you like to learn better ways to manage your feelings?
- Do you wish that you were better at making nice friends and keeping them?
- Do you sometimes feel really sad? Would you like to know what to do during those times?
- Do you ever feel bad about who you are and the things you do? Would you like to feel better about yourself?

If you said **YES** to any of these questions, this book is for you!

Taking on Your Behavior Challenge

If you *did* say yes to some of the questions, that means you probably deal with **behavior challenges.** Those behavior challenges are getting in the way of you being successful in school and getting along well with others there, at home, and in your neighborhood.

> **Words in black, bold type are explained in the glossary.**

Sometimes kids have such trouble making the right decisions that the schools decide they need to help by providing special support for those students. They give this help to kids who need it with **special education.** If your behavior challenge is very strong, adults at school might give you a label like **behavior disorder (BD)** so that they can give you extra special help. They do this because they know that with your best effort and their help, you can learn to make the right decisions on your own. When you've shown good choice-making for a long time, then the school knows that you are ready to be more in charge of your life. They'll give you more freedom in making choices, because you will have proven that you can manage your behavior. You've shown them that you are now ready to take control. (If you have a label like BD, you can read more about it and other labels in the special section near the end of the book, starting in section entitled "What If You Have Been Given a BD Label?".)

Whether you have a small, medium, or large behavior challenge, this book gives you the ideas and practice you need to help you take charge of your behavior and make wise decisions about how to act in different situations. This book gives you the answers to the following questions (and more):

- Why do kids with behavior challenges have trouble making good choices?
- What can kids with behavior challenges do about it?
- Why don't a lot of teachers, parents, and other kids understand kids who have behavior challenges?
- How can kids with behavior challenges make things better for themselves?

This book is full of ideas for learning to take charge of your own behavior so you can get along better with parents, other kids, and teachers. That's why the book has the title *The Survival Guide for Kids with Behavior Challenges.* "Survival" is when you keep going and make it through a tough experience. The book will talk about **challenges** a lot because that is what you face right now—challenges. These new challenges are like hurdles that runners jump over in some of their races. Right now, you're having trouble getting over them. As you read this book and do the activities, you will be training to jump over those hurdles. They seem very high right now, but you'll learn to leap over them. Then you'll practice what you've learned and keep improving. Soon, whenever you're in a situation that challenges you, you'll use your skills to get over those behavior hurdles. You'll feel proud of what you've done. And you'll be ready to run well in the race of life.

> **Kids live in many kinds of families. Maybe you live with one or two parents. Maybe you live with a foster parent, stepparent, guardian, relative, or other adult. This book usually says *parents, family adults,* or *adults at home.* When you see these words, think about the adult or adults you live with who take care of you.**

This book won't clear up all problems. But if you use its suggestions, it can make things **BETTER** for you in many ways. It can help you understand your behavior challenges better. It can give you ideas for making school and home better places to be. It can help you form better friendships. It can help you make smart behavior choices and feel better about yourself.

How to Use This Book

You can read this book a little at a time, or from start to finish. Or you can just read parts that are most interesting to you. You'll want to read some parts many times in order to better remember what to do in place of the old ways that aren't working too well for you.

Chapters 1–10 focus on helping you take charge of your behavior. You'll learn many skills for handling strong feelings and dealing with difficult people. You'll read and try ideas to help you get fair treatment from teachers. You'll learn ways to make and keep friends and get along at home, too.

At the back of the book, you'll find a special section talking about the label "BD." Here you'll find information about what it means to have an official label like BD, ED, EBD, or some other set of letters. You'll learn about the reasons some kids have behavior challenges or disorders. You'll read about the law that says schools are supposed to help kids with these challenges. You'll find out some ways schools work to do this.

In the book you will also find:

- **Stories and quotes** from real kids. These kids have faced challenges and choices because they have behavior challenges. (Their names have been changed for privacy reasons.)
- **"It's Your Turn"** questions. You will find these throughout this book. You might want to think or write about the questions and ideas in these boxes on your own. Or maybe you'll talk about them with a teacher, family adult, classmate, or friend.
- **"Idea!"** boxes. These suggest things you can do to help you make smart choices

- **"A Challenge for You"** activities. These will give you practice trying out new skills so that they become more comfortable and automatic.
- **Forms** you can copy or print out and use to keep track of your goals and progress. (If you want to write on the forms from this book, you can photocopy them, or you can print them out from the book publisher's website at www.freespirit.com/SG4K-behavior-forms. Use the password 4smartchoices.)
- Words you may need to know highlighted in **bold** type. Most of these words are explained the first time you read them. All of them are defined in the **glossary.**
- **A list** of books, organizations, and websites for learning more about many of the book's topics.
- The **index,** an alphabetical list of words and page numbers. The index is helpful if you want to find something very specific. For example, maybe in Chapter 5 you'll read about making a "sandwich." What if you don't remember what that's about? You can look for "sandwich" in the

index. The index will tell you the page numbers where the "sandwich" skill is explained. Then you can turn to those pages and read about it.

IDEA!

Keep a notebook or journal while you read this book. You can draw or write in it as you do the activities, or you can record whatever thoughts, feelings, and experiences come to mind. Maybe you'll have an idea to send to me!

Write to Dr. Mac

After you're done reading *The Survival Guide for Kids with Behavior Challenges,* please write to me. Let me know about the behavior challenges you have faced and how this book helps you. Tell me some ideas you have for dealing with behavior challenges. You can send a letter to me at this address:
Tom McIntyre
c/o Free Spirit Publishing
217 Fifth Avenue North, Suite 200
Minneapolis, MN 55401-1299

I like email, too! You can reach me that way at:

help4kids@freespirit.com

You have this book in your hands because someone believes that you have what it takes to make changes and make smart choices. That "someone" is there to support you in your efforts. If, by chance, you are reading this book alone and want to talk about it, ask an adult you trust to work with you. If you'd like to talk with me, the place to send letters and emails is mentioned above.

My best wishes for your success go out to you. Keep believing in yourself. And keep working on facing your challenges. If you do, someday you'll be able to look back and be really proud of what you've done.

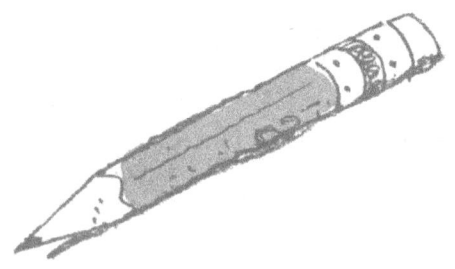

Dr. Mac

The Six Great Gripes of Kids with Behavior Challenges

Here are six things that bother a lot of kids who have behavior challenges:

1. Teachers, parents, and other kids don't like me for who I really am. The behavior keeps them from seeing the real me.
2. I don't have many friends.
   –OR–
   I wish that I had better friends who acted nicer.
3. Kids tease me. They call me names and make fun of the things I do.
4. Nobody explains to me what having behavior challenges is all about. Sometimes it makes me worry a lot. I wonder if something is wrong with me.
5. People only tell me when I'm doing things wrong. Even when I do the right thing, sometimes people don't notice.

6. It's really hard to change my behavior. I'm so used to acting in a certain way that I forget to use better ways.

With your hard work and the ideas in this book, these six gripes are going to go away. You can do it!

CHAPTER 1

Are You Ready?

If you're reading this book, adults have probably been telling you that your behavior needs to change. What do you think? Do you agree? A lot? A little? Not at all?

Psychologists have studied how people feel and act when they are told that changes need to be made. The experts say that most of us go through steps when we hear this news.

- When others tell us to change our ways, at first we usually don't see why we should have to do that.
- After a while, we notice that more people tell us we need to change our ways of behaving. Soon we begin to think maybe they are right. We begin to wonder if we should work on changing our actions. We also begin to wonder: If we *did* give it a try, would we be able to do it? Would we be successful?
- Next, we give the new ways a try. We practice them at home alone.

Then with someone else. Then we try to show these behaviors in some real situations that aren't too risky, like practicing with a brother, sister, or trusted adult at home or school. That way, if we don't do it quite right, it doesn't matter too much. We know we're just trying it out, and we know that we might not get it quite right until we practice more.

- Now that we've practiced the new ways, we decide we want to make a total change for the better. We try to remember to make the better choices all the time. We know that we might make mistakes, but we will learn from them and get better at using the new ways.

These steps might *sound* easy to do. They're not. They take courage. They take practice. They take patience. We especially need to be patient with ourselves when we make mistakes. Of course we're going to make mistakes. That's why they put erasers on pencils! Learning new behaviors is just like writing and erasing. We make mistakes, and then we make corrections and learn from our experience.

> **It helps to have one or two grown-ups work with you as you learn these new behavior choices. It also helps if these adults watch you and tell you which parts you did right, and how you can get better at these new ways. Adults can learn more about how to help you by going to this website:** www.BehaviorAdvisor.com/ReadinessForChange.html. **It talks about helping kids make smarter choices about their behavior.**

What's Your Starting Point?

Let's figure out where you're at right now. Take a look at the "Ready Ruler" form. Copy it or print it out online. Then make a mark on the Ready Ruler to show how you're feeling right now about your behavior. Answer honestly. Mark what you really think and feel inside yourself about whether you see a need to change your ways or not.

The closer your mark is to 0, the more you think that your usual ways of acting are okay, and the less you feel like you really need to change.

If your mark is in the middle range, you're thinking about maybe trying to change your behavior to what adults would like to see.

The closer your mark is to the number 10, the more convinced you are that you would like to work with someone who will help you change your behavior.

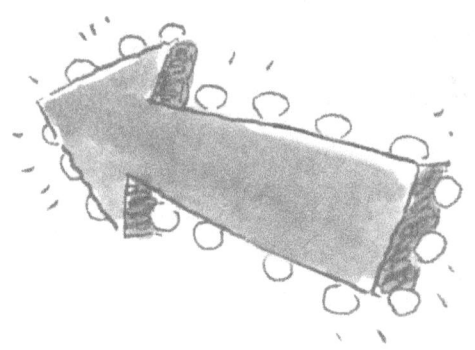

What to do now: Show your Ready Ruler to an adult you trust. Together, look at the next section and find the questions that are about the number where you placed your mark on the ruler. Talk about those questions with the adult.

If your mark is on numbers 0, 1, 2, or 3:

- What about your usual behavior leads you to keep doing it? How does it work well for you? What are the payoffs and benefits? What is working well for you?
- When you think about the behavior that adults would like you to show, why do you think it's not right for you?
- If you were going to change, what things about you MUST remain the same? In other words, what pieces of your personality and self are so important that they must remain a part of you? What should not change about you, no matter what, because it is an important part of who you are?
- Is there something about your thoughts, feelings, or personality that stops you from even thinking about changing?
- What would need to happen to get you thinking about changing the way you behave on a usual day? How will

you know when it is time to at least think about changing? What signs, situations, or happenings would convince you that you need to find new tools and new ways to live a better life?

If your mark is at 4, 5, or 6:

- Why did you put your mark here and not closer to zero? What makes you think about changing?
- What would you need in order to feel okay about moving your mark a little farther to the right?
- Have you tried some ways to change? What did you try? How well did it work for you? Did it work better than the old ways?
- If you tried some new ways to act in situations, but stopped, why did you stop? What do you think is better about your old ways than the new ways adults would like to see? (Or, if you don't use these new ways very often, why don't you use them more?)

- What gets in the way of changing? Why do you think change usually isn't quick or easy? What kind of support from others would help you with the changes you want to make?

If your mark is at 7, 8, 9, or 10:

- What would you like to talk about?
- Which behaviors would you like to change?
- What behaviors would you like to learn to show?
- What is the biggest hurdle to changing your behavior?
- What could help you overcome this hurdle?

After your discussion, make a second mark on the Ready Ruler that shows how you're feeling right now. Make this mark a different color or shape so that it doesn't get mixed up with the first one. Is it in the same place?

REMEMBER...
Change takes time—time and practice and patience and more

practice. At times, you may want to give up. But you won't. Why not? Because you want better things to happen in your life. You want others to be proud of you. You want to be proud of yourself.

Your journey to new ways of behaving is like climbing up a rocky hillside. You might slip back, but you'll keep trying. You might feel hurt at times. You might wonder if you're ever going to make it to the top. You will. Why? Because people are stronger than they think they are. Inside you are strengths that you haven't even discovered—yet!

Yes, that behavior hill looks scary at first, but you'll find your way up it. The view from the top is worth the difficult climb.

You are stronger than you think you are. You have what it takes to keep trying, even when the going gets tough. To quote Christopher Robin, the kid in the Winnie the Pooh stories: "You are braver than you believe, stronger than you seem, and smarter than you think."

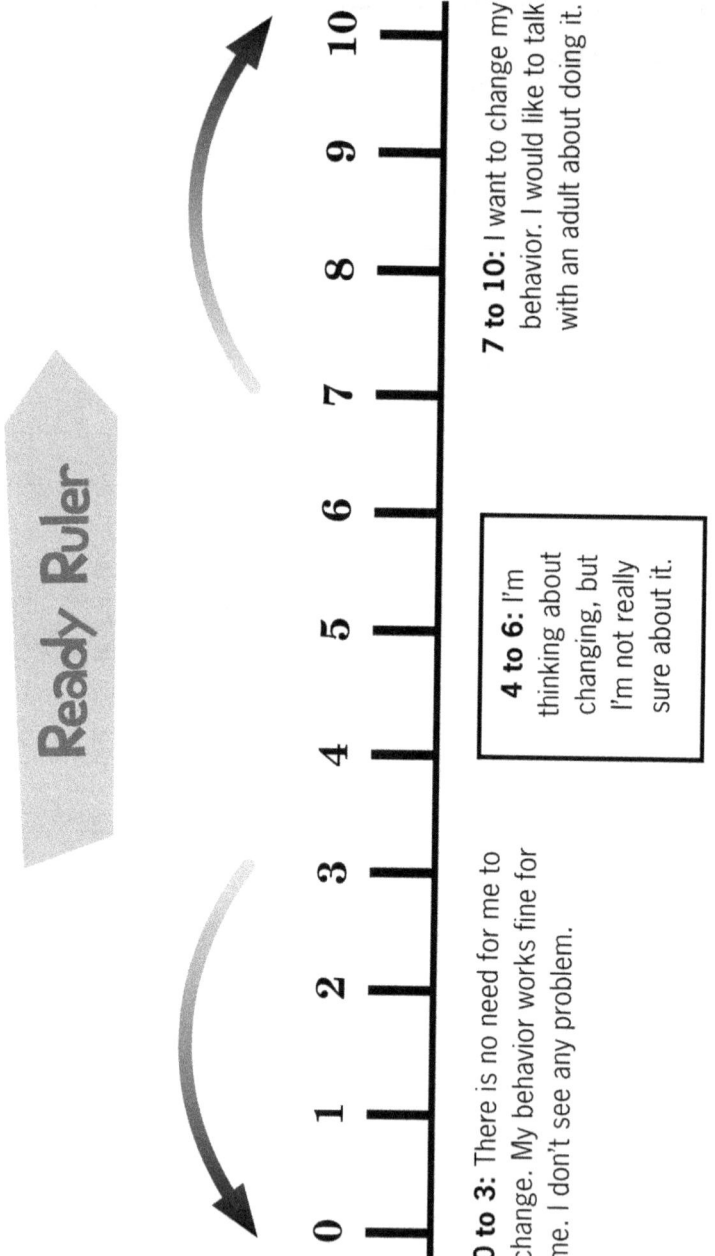

From *The Survival Guide for Kids with Behavior Challenges* by Tom

McIntyre, Ph.D., copyright © 2013. Free Spirit Publishing Inc., Minneapolis, MN; 800-735-7323; www.freespirit.com. This page may be reproduced for individual, classroom, or small group work only. For other uses, contact www.freespirit.com/company/permissions.cfm.

CHAPTER 2

Four Smart Choices for Dealing with Feelings

"My behavior is always getting me into trouble. It keeps me out of classes I want to be in, and other kids don't want to be around me. That hurts a lot. Sometimes, I get really angry and want to hurt those kids back. I get mad at myself, too. My choices are messing up my life." —C.J., 12

Being a kid with a behavior challenge is tough. I'm sure I'm not telling you anything you don't already know. You're under a lot of pressure to behave well. The work of trying to be good all the time can cause a lot of tension. It can be exhausting. Other people always seem to be telling you what you did wrong, or what you should be doing. Teachers, parents, and other kids may not see things the same way you do. When you make poor choices, people can get mad or decide they don't want to be around you. You might feel angry at people, at the choices you've made, and at yourself. You might feel **frustrated** or hurt, too.

With so much pressure, you can get pretty unhappy. This happens to many kids who have behavior challenges. It can seem like no one understands or cares about you. You might find that you're confused about your own feelings and behavior.

So what can you do when the pressure on you piles up too high? First, know that the feelings you have are okay. It's okay to feel sad or hurt or angry sometimes. It's also okay to have other strong, upset feelings—even if you don't know what exact feeling you have at the moment. Second, know that you always have choices about how to *deal* with strong emotions. You can learn to make smart choices instead of ones that only make the problem worse.

How Can I Tell the Difference Between a Bad Choice and a Smart One?

There's usually an easy way to tell the difference:
- Bad choices bring on more **stress** and more bad feelings. They make things worse than they were.
- Smart choices get rid of the stress and bring better feelings. They make things better.

Bad Choices

People who make bad choices when they have strong feelings often do it in one or more of these ways:

Acting without thinking. Someone who does this feels the emotion and just says or does something right away. This isn't really a choice because the person does not think about what to do. But with practice, this person can learn to control that behavior and think before acting.

Thinking in a negative way. Sometimes people think before they act, but they don't think in helpful ways. Instead, they think about the stressful thing over and over. Their emotions keep getting stronger and stronger. Finally, a person in this situation will feel ready to burst. Then the person acts up.

Losing control. Kids who make no decisions or bad ones about handling emotions may lose control. They might do things like:
- hit themselves or others
- throw things (or destroy them)

- curse or say bad things to themselves or others
- refuse to do work or follow directions
- walk out of class or put their heads down on the tabletop or desk

Some kids cry when their emotions get too strong. This is a lot better than doing something wrong. But these kids can learn to think about things differently and act in control so that crying doesn't happen so often or so strongly.

You Always Have a Choice

You can choose whether or not to let something bother you. And you can choose how *much* you'll let it bother you. The amount of stress you feel, and how you react to it, depends on how much attention you decide to give a bad feeling or a difficult situation. And *you* are the one who decides whether to make wrong choices or smart ones.

What happens when kids act on their feelings without thinking about how to handle them? They are no longer in charge of themselves. They're letting their feelings control them. When kids keep thinking about someone or something until they burst out with negative behaviors, they're letting others be in charge of them.

YOU'RE SMARTER THAN THAT!

You don't want to be "controlled" in these ways. The good news is this: You can learn ways to handle your emotions and make good decisions when the pressure starts to build up. No, it's not easy to make smart choices when your feelings get really strong. Yes, it takes practice to learn new and better ways to help yourself. But **YOU CAN DO IT!**

Smart Choices

When your feelings build up, it's important to talk to yourself about what's happening. You need to figure out whether you really want to let some person or thing give you stress and negative feelings. This book gives you new ways to think about what happened, and new ways to make smart choices in tense situations.

There are many ways to help deal with your feelings and make better choices. Here are five important ways:

1. **Build your self-esteem** (how good you feel about yourself). Then things won't bother you as much. You'll feel confident about yourself and think about how to react calmly in difficult situations.

> This chapter will explain the first four ways to make smart choices...

2. **Talk with someone you trust.** The person can listen and help you work out a plan of action for handling the troubling situation.
3. **Write, draw, or paint.** Use writing or art to express how you feel. Doing this can help you express your feelings and think about how to handle them in a productive way.
4. **Chill out or get moving!** Relaxation and exercise can go a long way to ease strong feelings. They give you time to think about what to do next.
5. **Stop, think, choose, and think again.** Getting in the habit of doing these steps can help you through many tough times.

> ...Chapter 3 explains the fifth way.

Read about each of these ways. Decide which ones would work best for you. Then try them out.

IMPORTANT!

Everybody feels angry, sad, and stressed sometimes. These feelings are part of being human. Sometimes, though, these feelings are extra-strong for kids who have behavior challenges. The ideas in Chapters 2 and 3 can help. But maybe you have strong, upset, or sad feelings all the time. Or maybe you feel like hurting yourself or someone else. Maybe you're afraid someone else is going to hurt you. If any of these things are true for you, get help right away. Here are three ways to get help:

- Talk to an adult you trust.
- Look in the Yellow Pages under Crisis Intervention.
- Call the toll-free National Youth Crisis Hotline at 1-800-448-4663 or 1-800-442-4673.

SMART CHOICE #1: Build Your Self-Esteem

Kids who have behavior challenges want to get rid of them right away. But getting rid of these challenges takes time and hard work. Having behavior challenges can make kids feel bad about themselves. Sometimes their **self-esteem** is low. Often they forget about all the good things they do and about how they are getting better at making good choices. It's important for kids with behavior challenges to remember these positive things. Be proud of what you do well! Also, take pride in the things you are doing better now than before.

IT'S YOUR TURN

Make a list of things you do well (or are getting better at doing). What things about YOU should you take pride in? (Remember, you can write your answers to these questions on your own, or talk about them with someone. It's up to you.)

Do "Pride and Progress" Exercises

It's important to take **pride** in things that you do well. It's also important to notice when you are getting better at doing things. That shows **progress.** You can remember to notice those strong skills you have and keep getting better at others. How? By doing "pride and progress" exercises each day. These aren't exercises for your body (even though those can help self-esteem, too). They are exercises for your mind. The "pride" part lets you notice things you like about yourself. The "progress" part lets you notice smart choices. Here's how to do these exercises. **(They' re fun!)**

In the morning
1. Start the day by talking to yourself. Look in the mirror and give yourself a big, happy "Good morning!" (Or maybe a nod or simple thumbs-up.)
2. Say **one** thing you like about yourself. (After a few days, say two or three things.)
3. Tell yourself the ways that you're improving. Brag to yourself.
4. Set a goal for today. Tell yourself the good choice you will make happen today.

5. Imagine the times during the day when it might be hard to meet your goal. Think of people and places that might lead you to wrong choices. Think about what you will say and do to avoid those negative influences and to be sure

that you meet (or exceed) your goal.

During the day
1. Think about your goal every time you enter a new room. Think about it before you enter the bus or hallway or playground, too. Get yourself ready to do well in each of the places you enter.
2. Compliment yourself during the day. Congratulate yourself for doing well on meeting a goal in a class. You don't have to do this in a mirror. You can say it in your head. Be sure to say something nice to yourself when you make a right choice anytime during the day.

At night
1. End the day with "mirror talking" again. Look in the mirror and report on how well you did.
2. Talk about the times when you made good choices today. Smile. Give yourself a thumbs-up or high five.
3. Talk about the times when things went wrong during the day. Don't let these things bother you again.

Just make a report to yourself. What bad choices did you make? Don't blame others. You have to learn to make good choices even when other people do things you don't like. What mistakes did **YOU** make?

4. Think about the choices you **should** have made when things went wrong. In your mind, see yourself doing things differently and making smarter choices.
5. Make a promise to yourself to do things better tomorrow. Set a goal (or two) for the next day. (You'll say the goal again tomorrow morning when you get ready for school.) Now the day is done. You can't change what happened. Let

your mind rest, say "Good night," and get a good night's sleep.

Pride and progress exercises feel good. They also make your mind stronger so that things bother you less. Then it won't hurt so much if people tease or **criticize** you. The stress from the hard work of trying to behave better won't be so strong. When you know and remember the good things about yourself, you'll be able to manage your behavior challenges better.

Do these exercises each morning and night. On the weekends, set goals for getting along better at home and with the people in your neighborhood. Take pride in your progress. Of course, you'll still make mistakes. But you are getting better at working with people and handling frustration. If you mess up, be honest about it and work on your goals again. **Never give up.** You'll get there.

David

David is working on self-esteem with his counselor, Mr. Jones. Mr. Jones asks David to say something good about himself. David says, "I'm great at electronic games."

"Anything other than those games?" Mr. Jones asks.

"I'm good at taking care of my dog and fixing things that break."

The counselor says, "Great. The games show that you have good attention and good eye-hand coordination. Helping with the dog and fixing things show responsibility, patience, and caring. What goal are you working on right now?"

"Asking before taking something," says David.

"How are you doing at meeting your goal?" asks Mr. Jones.

"Sometimes I remember, but I still forget, too," says David.

Mr. Jones tells David that remembering the goal some of the time shows progress: It's better than not remembering at all. He says that David is starting to make better decisions. The counselor reminds David to think of the goal before going into each classroom. He also reminds him to do his pride and progress exercises.

IT'S YOUR TURN

If you haven't practiced "mirror talking" before, you can practice it with another person who knows what it is. This person can read the book if he or she needs to understand mirror talking better. Have the person watch and listen while you do it. Ask the person to tell you what you did well, and where you can improve. Try it again, working to include those improvements.

At home that evening, David walks to his bedroom mirror and looks in it. He feels strange about talking to the mirror. He thinks, "This is dumb." But he wants to make better decisions and handle stress better. He has trouble looking at himself. But each time his head drops down, he looks up again. Finally, David says "hi" in a soft voice. Then he goes through all the nighttime steps.

Start a "Helping Habit"

Have you ever noticed how good you feel when you do something that makes another person happy? Giving a helping hand to others is a great way to start building your own self-esteem. Make it a habit! We often think of habits as bad things. But it's **GOOD**—for others and for you—when you get into a "helping habit." Look for opportunities to help others and to do nice things for people.

Sandra

One day at school, Sandra was walking behind two kids carrying boxes of supplies to a classroom down the hall. One of the students lost her grip on the box and it fell to the floor. Pencils and pens rolled all over the place. Notebooks spilled out. Sandra stopped and helped the girl put the things back in the box. Sandra's help was appreciated by the other student, it made Sandra feel warm inside, and it even brought a smile to the face of a teacher standing by the door to his classroom. As Sandra reached her classroom door, she thought about her goal for the day. She wanted that warm feeling of pride again.

Mo and Tina

Mo and Tina saw Mrs. Hassett, one of their neighbors, drive her car into the parking lot behind their apartment building. There were lots of bags and boxes in the car. They stopped their checkers game and walked toward Mrs. Hassett. She accepted their offer to help her bring the things into her apartment and said, "Thank you so much!" Bringing the items up to the apartment earned Tina and Mo another thank you. They also got a couple of pieces of fruit to share. Afterward, Mo and Tina both felt proud about being good neighbors. Helping out took only a few minutes, but the good feeling lasted a lot longer.

The stories about Sandra, Mo, and Tina show that there are easy ways to be helpful. You can look for chances to show kindness to others in school, at home, and in your neighborhood. Do good deeds for no reason. Notice how you feel about yourself when you do these kind and generous acts.

Here are some "kindly" things you might do. You can probably think of more:
- Volunteer when your teacher asks for someone to pass out papers, reorganize a classroom shelf, or clean off the board.
- Notice someone who seems lonesome or left out of the activities of others. Say hi and talk for a minute. Invite the person to sit with you during lunch.
- Listen when a friend is mad or sad. Help them make a positive plan of action.
- Surprise your sister (or brother) by making her (or his) bed.
- Make a nice card for your parent, uncle or aunt, grandparent, or cousin.
- Give someone a compliment about something they did well (or tried hard to do).
- When you sit down in class, smile at the person next to you who you don't know very well and say hi.

IDEA!

In your journal or notebook, make a large calendar page. Make the box for each day large enough to write a few words inside. Each night, write down one nice thing that you did for someone that day. If you can't remember anything, think of something that you can do for your family right now. Can you wash some dishes, take out the trash, fold some clothes, read a book to a younger sister or brother, or pick up a mess ... even if you didn't make it? Once you do that thing, write it in that date's box. Start thinking about something nice you can do for someone tomorrow. Don't forget to compliment yourself each day for your kindness to others!

SMART CHOICE #2: Talk with Someone You Trust

Jessie

Jessie had trouble making smart choices when her feelings got really strong. If things went well at home in the morning, she was all smiles. She would be in a great mood when she came to school. But there were things in Jessie's life that sometimes caused a lot of pressure and strong, unhappy feelings. When she had troubles at home, she would come to school upset. She would act up in class and sometimes hurt others. The teachers punished Jessie for doing these things. Then she would get even more upset and act worse.

Jessie was sent to talk with a school counselor. The counselor helped Jessie understand her feelings better. Jessie talked with the counselor about the strong emotions she felt. She wanted to make better choices so she would stay out of trouble. The counselor helped her figure out ways to respond in those upsetting times. Jessie talked to the teacher in her special class, too. The teacher decided to work with Jessie (and the other kids with behavior challenges) on **anger management.** They practiced better ways to think about the situations, and new ways they could act even when their feelings got to be too much.

Over time, Jessie made more and more smart choices. And she made fewer and fewer poor choices when she was under stress. She got better at dealing with strong feelings. As she did this, things improved a little at home. But not much. Even so, Jessie became a lot better at handling her feelings and making the right choices even when she felt a lot of pressure.

When a person can't talk with someone about being angry or sad, those feelings can stay around. Often, they get stronger. The person keeps feeling confused, hurt, or mad. Then it's hard to enjoy doing things or being with people. It's hard to do schoolwork and follow directions. It's hard to think about anything but those bad feelings.

Teachers care about you. Yes, they do! (They care even at times when some of them have a hard time managing their own feelings.) They want to help you deal better with your feelings. Many schools also have counselors who are trained to help kids talk about their feelings and find better ways to handle them. If you would like to talk with a counselor, ask your teacher to introduce you. You can do this even if you're not sure how you're feeling or what to say. Counselors can help you make sense of things and feel better.

A friend who really cares about you can be another helpful person to talk to. If you have a friend like this, that's great. It can still be a good idea to find an adult to talk things over with as well. If your school doesn't have a counselor, maybe you can talk to a grown-up at home. Or maybe there's another adult you can talk to. It should be someone you trust to listen to your feelings, offer some good advice, and keep things private. Choose carefully and wisely.

IDEA!

Think of some people you know who might be good "counselors"—people you would trust to listen to you and talk about feelings. For each person you think of, ask yourself:

- Am I comfortable talking honestly with this person about myself?
- Is the person wise?
- Does the person listen well?
- Can I trust this person to keep our conversation private (or to share it only with adults who can help)?

If the answers to the questions are all yes, this may be a good person to talk to. In your notebook or journal, make a list of the adults and friends who can be "counselors" when you need help with feelings.

Adults You Might Talk To

1. a parent
2. a stepparent
3. a foster parent
4. an aunt
5. an uncle
6. a grandparent
7. a counselor
8. a teacher
9. a coach
10. a principal
11. a doctor
12. a nurse
13. your friend's parent

14. a neighbor you know well
15. a scout or club leader
16. a leader at your place of worship

17. a psychologist or therapist
18. a social worker
19. a sitter
20. a family friend

or maybe your dog (Your furry friend won't say anything back to you, but many dogs make great listeners!)

SMART CHOICE #3: Write or Draw

If you don't have someone to talk to about feelings (or just don't want to talk), there are other ways that can help you sort things out. One way is by writing in your journal or notebook. You could write something short, or something long. You could write a poem or a song. You could write a letter to yourself or someone else. You could write a story. Or you could write words that describe how you feel or how you'd like to feel.

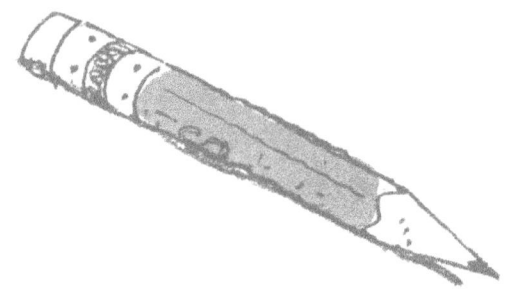

Maybe writing isn't your "thing." You can also draw pictures that show how you feel. If you find a trustworthy person (or if you do eventually feel like talking), you can show that person your drawings. This will help him or her understand what you are going through.

SMART CHOICE #4: Chill Out or Get Moving!

Sometimes, even when we try our best to manage our emotions, they can start to get out of control. Maybe you're working on some of the ways you read about in this chapter, but you're not really good at using them yet. (You will be, with more practice.) In the meantime, what can you do if you really start to get mad, hurt, or sad?

IT'S YOUR TURN

Even while you are still learning new smart choices from this book, you can be making them, thinking about them, and getting better at them every day.

- **What smart choices did you make in the last couple of days? You can be proud of those. Tell yourself, "Hey, great job!"**
- **Which choices were not so good because they caused problems or made problems worse? What could you have done instead?**

Practice that better choice right now. Really! Pretend that you are back in that situation. Then say or act out the right behavior. This practice will help you remember to make better choices in the future.

Just stop what you're doing and *relax.* When your thoughts and feelings seem to be too much to handle, close your eyes and take some slow, deep breaths through your nose. Breathe **D-E-E-P-L-Y.** Then let out the air from your mouth in a "Whoosh!" Next, bring into your mind some thoughts or memories of nice things. You might think of being with friends. Or about a trip you took to a favorite place, or doing your favorite activity. If those wonderful thoughts slip away, work to bring them back.

See if you can move your hands, arms, and head in a slow, relaxed way. Your arms and neck should feel like wet noodles. If they feel stiff, start taking those deep breaths again. Think those good thoughts again. Calm yourself until you are ready to get back into the situation. Before you get back into things, make a positive plan for how you will act in that situation. Then congratulate yourself on controlling your feelings.

Another way to handle a pile of negative or confused feelings is to get moving! Exercise may seem like the opposite of relaxing. But it is another good way to help calm a mind filled with strong feelings. If you're in a sad or upset mood, exercise can help you let out those emotions. You don't have to keep your feelings inside you till you feel like you want to burst. Instead, you can help them "escape" as you run, jump, do push-ups, shoot baskets, ride a bike, or dance.

IT'S YOUR TURN

Practice the breathing and the positive thinking you just read about. If it helps, you can lie down and close your eyes to get used to breathing slowly to relax. With practice, you'll be able to relax sitting or standing in other situations, too. Perhaps an adult could use a relaxation talk to lead you through the relaxation process. Many examples are online.

REMEMBER...

It's important to feel good about who you are and to learn to be in control of your feelings. Building your self-esteem can help you make better choices. So can talking to people who can help, writing or drawing, relaxing, and getting exercise. When you make those better choices, you'll be on your way to overcoming your behavior challenges.

But wait, there's more! Read Chapter 3 for one more smart

choice that can help you take charge of your feelings and how you handle them.

CHAPTER 3

Another Smart Choice for Dealing with Feelings

"I'm not fighting like before or cursing at the teachers. I've calmed my attitude down." —Amber, 12

Sometimes what you do to try to make things better doesn't work. At other times, you might choose to keep quiet, but you still feel upset. You might feel very angry at someone. You might be frustrated at not being able to do something well. You might be sad because someone did or said something that hurt you. You might want to hurt that person back. You feel the stress building up. These are the times when it's easy to make a wrong choice about behavior.

In Chapter 2 you learned four smart choices for handling your feelings at such times. But what if the situation calls for something different? You might not be home in front of a mirror. There may not be someone there **RIGHT NOW** who you trust to listen and understand. You might not be able to write or draw or relax or get moving. That's when it's time for another smart choice. It's called "Stop, Think, Choose, and Think Again."

SMART CHOICE #5: Stop, Think, Choose, and Think Again

When you're in a tough situation and feeling upset, you need a plan. What can you do to make things better? How can you avoid a bad decision, and make a good one? Follow these four steps:

STOP. The first thing is to be sure that you don't do anything you'll **regret** later. Tell yourself, "Stop!" Don't do anything! Don't say anything! Just stand or sit and be quiet.

"Regret" means you did something, but later you wish you hadn't—but by then, it's too late to take it back.

THINK. The next thing to do is calm your mind, getting rid of all those negative feelings and thoughts about what just happened. Then think about what's going on and how you need to come up with a positive way to react. This can help you sort things out and make better choices. To do this kind of thinking, use **self-talk**—talk to yourself.

Ask yourself, "What is the problem?" Think about different ways to handle it. Each way is a possible choice. For each choice, think about what could or will happen. Ask yourself:

CHOOSE. After thinking about the different things you could do right now, choose the one that has the **most** good reasons with the **fewest** chances of getting you in trouble or making things worse.

THINK AGAIN. After you have followed your choice, think again. Ask yourself:

Keeping Calm Can Help

You always have a choice about what you decide to do. Your decision will depend on the situation.

Paulo

Paulo looks at the worksheet his teacher just gave to him. Miss O'Hara said it was easy. Even so, Paulo doesn't remember what to do. He tries to figure it out, but he gets frustrated. He remembers the right thing to do when he gets stuck: He asks for help. But Miss O'Hara says, "Keep going. You can do it."

This bothers Paulo. Miss O'Hara thinks Paulo ought to be able to do it, but Paulo can't remember how. He wonders if he is dumb. He tries again. The work just doesn't make sense. The stress gets even stronger. He keeps thinking about how Miss O'Hara didn't help him. Then Paulo makes a bad choice. He yells out, "I can't do this stuff! I need help!" Instead of giving him help, Miss O'Hara gives him a warning. And she tells Paulo to get back to work.

Paulo is about to curse at his teacher. But then he remembers "Stop, Think, Choose, and Think Again." He has practiced doing this with other kids in his anger management group and on his own when he takes care of his younger brother. He **STOPS** himself. He knows swearing will get him punished. He says silently to himself, "Keep cool. Think about what to do."

Then Paulo **THINKS.** The first thing that comes to his mind is to rip up the paper. That would show how angry he is! But he knows it will get him punished. (And how can he learn the stuff if the paper is ripped up?) Then he thinks about walking out of the room. He could go see Mrs. Lee, the special ed teacher who always helps him. But if he walks out now, he'll get in trouble. Paulo keeps trying to figure out how to handle this situation.

After thinking some more, Paulo **CHOOSES** what to do. He decides to put his name and the date at the top of the paper. He pretends to work. When the bell rings for lunch, he hands in the paper.

At lunch, Paulo **THINKS AGAIN** about what happened. He knows Miss O'Hara didn't like the way he yelled in class. He also worries about what she will do when she sees that Paulo didn't complete the work. He doesn't know how to get the help he needs. He decides to visit Mrs. Lee. He gets a pass to do this during recess. She says she will talk to Miss O'Hara about the learning help Paulo needs. Paulo says he will stick with his choice to stay calm and polite.

The next day, Paulo apologizes to Miss O'Hara for yelling out in class. Miss O'Hara smiles and says, "That's okay. Just don't let it happen again."

Paulo is disappointed. He thinks, "This isn't fair. Where's my apology?" He wants to tell the teacher, "You should say you're sorry, too." Paulo keeps thinking about this. He feels the stress build up. Then he remembers to tell himself to "Stop!" He goes to his desk. He starts to use self-talk again to keep from saying something wrong. Getting in trouble isn't worth it.

Did you notice how Paulo stayed cool even when he was frustrated? He didn't get the help or the apology he wanted from Miss O'Hara. But he kept himself out of trouble just the same. He stopped. He thought about ways to act. He made choices about what to do. He found some help from Mrs. Lee. And he decided to just forget that Miss O'Hara didn't apologize. Heck, if she needed to learn better manners, that was her problem—not his. Paulo did the right thing. He should congratulate himself for staying calm, being polite, and making good choices.

Mali

Mali and Linda are friends from the same neighborhood. But Linda sometimes does things that aren't very nice. She sometimes tells Mali's secrets to others. Once in a while at lunch, Linda sits with the popular kids and ignores Mali. At times, she blames things on Mali. Then Mali gets punished instead of her. When Mali finds out about these things, she becomes really angry! She yells at Linda and threatens her. One time she even threw things at Linda. When this happened, the teacher saw it. Mali got in trouble and was sent to the principal.

Mr. Williams, the school's counselor, is working with Mali to help her handle her anger better. He gives her and some other students lessons in anger management. It has taken a while, but Mali is making progress. Now, when Linda is not such a good friend, Mali remembers to **STOP** and **THINK**. She says, "I'll talk with you later. I have something I need to do right now." Using calm words is a smart **CHOICE** for Mali. Linda apologizes when she hears Mali's words. She knows she has hurt her friend. Later, Mali **THINKS AGAIN.** She plans more things she can do and say in other situations that start to get her mad. She is also thinking about ways she can talk to Linda about their friendship. She wants to be friends, but not if Linda keeps hurting her.

Mali made a plan for what to say in situations that happened a lot. She thought ahead about some words she could use.

IDEA!

Ask your school counselor or **special education** teacher to start an **anger management** group to help kids make better choices when they get upset. (Section entitled "What About Resources for Grown-Ups?" tells where schools can find a list of books and websites to help kids with anger and conflict management.)

Using "Ready Replies"

When it comes to figuring out what to say, there are good and bad choices. The bad ones are angry words like insults. They make the situation worse. The good ones give you the chance to defend yourself without making things worse. Good choices show respect. They leave some room to solve the problem. You can think of these good responses as "ready replies." By planning ahead, you'll be able to use these helpful words when you need them.

Here are some examples of wrong words kids with behavior challenges might be tempted to say, and ready replies they could plan to say instead:

WRONG WORDS

To a teacher
- "I don't get this stuff because you don't teach it right! How come I got stuck with such a crummy teacher?"

To another kid
- "If you think I'm so stupid, why don't you go sit somewhere else? You're the one who's stupid!"

To a family adult
- "All you ever do is criticize me and find fault with what I do. I hate you!"

READY REPLY

- "Could you please explain it again? Or could you help me during lunch?"

- "You can move somewhere else if you want. But I know that I'm not stupid, and anyone who says that should probably take a closer look in the mirror."

- "I wish you'd also notice when I do something right. I make lots of good decisions, too."

A Challenge for You

Read the challenge and look at the choices. Think about what might happen if Sam decides to make each of these choices. Choose the ones that let him handle the situation without causing more problems or getting in trouble. Write down the numbers. (When you're done, you can compare your choices to the solutions in section entitled "Solutions to Some of the Challenges and Questions".)

When you see "A Challenge for You," get out your pencil and notebook. These fun exercises will help you practice the new skills you're learning.

CHALLENGE: A couple of boys pass by Sam. They say a bad thing about his mother. Which choices are smart ones for Sam?

1. Sam says something nasty about *their* mothers.

2. Sam says, "I don't play the mother insult game."

3. Sam chases and hits one of the boys.

4. Sam thinks, "They can't be talking about my mom. She's super!" He ignores them.

5. Sam thinks, "That really hurts. I hate it when they say these things. But if I get upset, they'll do it more. I'll say, 'I don't have time for this nonsense.' Then I'll walk away."

6. Sam says, "Come on, guys, quit talking about others and worry about yourselves."

7. Sam says nothing. Later, he talks with his friend Louis about how much it hurts to hear these things.

8. Sam says, "You've got the wrong mom," and keeps walking. He ignores the next few comments until he is away from the other boys.

Thinking About Solutions

When you're using "Stop, Think, Choose, and Think Again," ready replies are things you can **CHOOSE.** They give you one way of making a choice that won't hurt—and might help. Often, you will have to think of some other solutions to problem situations.

IT'S YOUR TURN

Think of a time when someone said something mean or upsetting to you. Maybe the person called you a name. Or maybe somebody made fun of you for being in special ed.

- What did you do? Did you just stay quiet? Did you say something angry back?
- What ready reply could you have said instead?

Plan to use that ready reply the next time this happens!

Jasmine

Jasmine moved to her new school from far away. She had an accent and said some words differently from people in her new town. She used words that the other kids did not know, and she didn't understand a lot of expressions that the kids at school used. Some of her new classmates said she talked funny. Jasmine didn't like to hear this. She also got upset when kids laughed at her way of speaking.

Jasmine wanted to shout: "What a bunch of losers!" But before she did this, she stopped herself. She thought, "I don't want to cause trouble. And I don't want to make things worse at my new school." So Jasmine made a smart choice: She decided not to say anything back. But Jasmine kept thinking about those comments. She felt really hurt by them. She cried about them a lot when she was by herself. At school, Jasmine felt lonely. She was embarrassed to talk. At home, she felt sad and angry. She realized it was time to think again about how to handle her situation. She had done the right thing when she chose not to yell at the kids and call them names. But she needed to do something else, too.

Jasmine thought that if she spoke more like the other kids, the teasing would probably slowly stop. She decided to pay attention to how people at her new school said things. When she was alone, she started practicing the new ways to talk. Soon, she could say some things in two different ways. That felt good. Plus, she was getting in the habit of speaking more like the other kids when they were around.

This seemed to work some of the time. Quite a few of the kids stopped teasing. But there were still some kids who remembered the old way Jasmine had spoken. They kept picking on her about it. In her special class, Jasmine and the other students had been learning about good and bad replies. She thought about a good ready reply that she could say the next time someone teased her. In front of the mirror, she practiced smiling and saying it: "Yeah. We say things in different ways where I come from. I want to learn your way, too. How do you say that word here?"

Jasmine also decided on what to do if some kids kept teasing her anyway and she felt bothered. She would ask her teacher to please do something to stop these comments.

IDEA!

Think about hard situations that seem to keep happening in school. For each situation, come up with a ready reply you can say. Write these replies in your notebook or journal. (If you wish, copy and use the "Ready Replies" planning.) Practice them. You could do this alone in front of the mirror. Or you could practice with a friend, a trusted adult at school, or someone in your family. T hen, the next time something happens that usually leads to problems, you'll be prepared!

> ### IT'S YOUR TURN
>
> **Practice "Stop, Think, Choose, and Think Again." Find someone you trust. Have the person say or do some things that you sometimes get mad about. Practice each step. Talk together about how different choices might work. Write some of the good ideas you have in your notebook or journal. Next time you're really in a situation like the one you practiced, try doing one of the choices you figured out.**

REMEMBER...

Everybody gets upset at times. It's normal. When your feelings are really strong, it's easy to make the wrong choices. But you can handle things a better way! "Stop, Think, Choose, and Think Again" is a skill that can help you do this. Practice, keep trying, and don't give up! No one can promise that this skill will make your life

> perfect. But things WILL be better for you. REALLY!

Ready Replies

Make some copies of this planning form to keep in your desk, notebook, or locker. Keep some at home, too. Use a form each time you want to plan ahead about what to say in a tough situation.

For Now

1. What is one thing people say or do that you don't like? Write it here:

[Space left intentionally blank in original book]

2. What ready reply can you say next time someone says or does that thing? Write your ready reply here:

[Space left intentionally blank in original book]

For Later

After you have tried using the words you planned, answer questions 3–6.

3. Did your reply help the situation? _____ Yes _____ No

4. If YES, that's great! Keep that ready reply in mind. Use it again!

5. If NOT, what was the problem?

_____ I got the words wrong.

_____ I should have used a different voice.

_____ The person didn't listen to what I said.

_____ The person made fun of what I said.

_____ Other (write the problem here):

[Space left intentionally blank in original book]

6. If there was a PROBLEM, what can you say or do next time? Write how you'll change what you say or how you say it:

[Space left intentionally blank in original book]

From *The Survival Guide for Kids with Behavior Challenges* by Tom McIntyre, Ph.D., copyright © 2013. Free Spirit Publishing Inc., Minneapolis, MN; 800-735-7323; www.freespirit.com. This page may be reproduced for individual, classroom, or small group work only.

For other uses, contact www.freespirit.com/company/permissions.cfm.

CHAPTER 4

Three Survival Skills for Dealing with Difficult People

"I found out that kids picked on me to see me react. But since I started ignoring the comments that used to make me mad, things are getting better." —Trina, 9

It's really hard to control your feelings around "difficult" people. Difficult people can do lots of irritating things. How do you keep from getting upset?

First, remember those smart choices from Chapters 2 and 3.

Second, think about what **YOU** can control. Can you control what other people say or do? No. Can you control how you respond? **YES.** You decide what you say, do, or tell yourself. You might feel hurt or angry about what someone says. But no one can "make" you yell, hit, or say awful things back. If you do something mean or hurt someone back, you aren't staying in charge of your own actions. That means you're letting someone else take charge of you. You want to be the captain of your behavior boat.

That old way of reacting can get you into trouble. It's not a smart choice. It won't help you feel good about yourself. It won't help you get along with other kids or adults. And it won't let **YOU** take control.

So don't give your power away to others. Instead, use the power you have to help yourself! There are lots of ways to stay in charge. Many kids have learned smart choices to make when others do things that aren't right. You can learn them, too. This chapter will show you three powerful skills you can use to deal with people who are difficult. Practice these skills and get in the habit of using them. They'll help you **survive** and take control in all kinds of tough situations.

1. Ignore Mean Words and Actions

Sometimes, the best thing to do is to ignore nasty comments and other kids' bothersome behavior. This is easy to say, and hard to do. But you can do it. How?

First, stop yourself before you make a bad choice. Cool yourself down with self-talk. (You can read more about self-talk in Chapter 3,.) While you ignore others, it helps to tell yourself things like this:

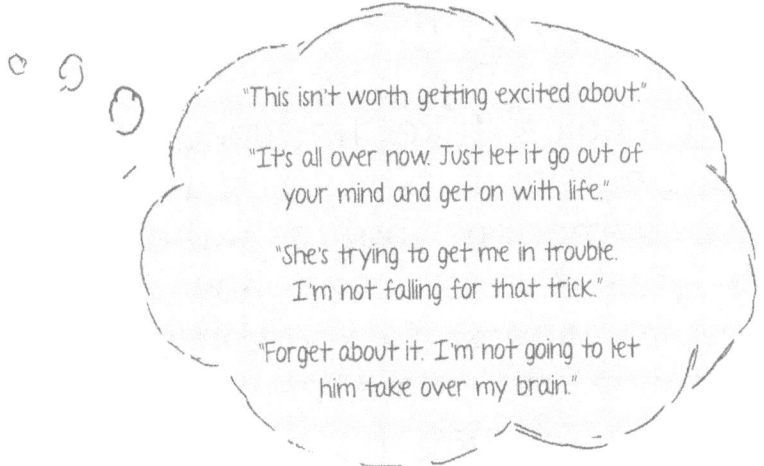

"This isn't worth getting excited about."

"It's all over now. Just let it go out of your mind and get on with life."

"She's trying to get me in trouble. I'm not falling for that trick."

"Forget about it. I'm not going to let him take over my brain."

Ask yourself, "What else can I think about?" Maybe you'll think about what you should be doing right then. Or about a song or game you like. Or just about something nice.

Don't take it personally. When people say or do something mean or unkind, understand that **THEY** have a problem. They are filled with bad feelings. Why let this become a problem for you, too? Don't let someone else's wrong choice take up space in your head. Shut your mind to it. If someone keeps bothering you, call the teacher over. Tell the teacher how you are trying to ignore the person. Say that you could use some help in handling this difficult situation.

> IT'S YOUR TURN
> - What are some things you can do or think about when someone is trying to upset you?

> • **What are some ways you can stay calm and ignore the person?**
> **After you think of some ways, have someone you trust say or do unkind or annoying things to you. Remember that this is your chance to practice handling these situations better. Keep cool. Practice the new ways of staying calm and ignoring these things.**

Keep at it. When you first ignore someone, the person is probably going to do more of the same thing. You'll have to keep ignoring the behavior. This will be hard. The person may say and do more mean things to get you to pay attention. Keep ignoring this. Sooner or later, the person will think, "Hmmm, this doesn't work anymore." Then the person will finally stop. But if you give in and say "Shut up" or another mean thing back, you're giving the other person control over you. Then you'll just keep having problems in the future.

Ignoring means **NO** attention at all. None. This means that you look somewhere else and notice things that take your mind off that difficult person. No rolling your eyes, making faces, or giving dirty looks. You just want to put on a calm face and go about your business.

IMPORTANT!

Ignoring may not always be a smart choice if the difficult person you're dealing with is an **authority figure.** Often, ignoring a teacher or parent will just get you in trouble. Instead, you can use the next two survival skills in this chapter. Chapters 5, 6, 8, and 9 also have lots of ideas to help you solve problems with teachers and family adults.

2. Be Assertive

Sometimes you need to tell others that you don't like what they have done. Maybe the teacher blamed you for something that wasn't your fault. Maybe your parent told you to do something you don't think you should have to do. Maybe another student took something of yours without asking.

When these things happen, it's time to be **assertive.**

People who are assertive speak up, in a strong but polite way. They don't use a harsh voice or angry words. They don't try to solve problems by shouting, fighting, or saying awful things about someone else. (Shouting and angry words make things worse, not better.) And assertive people don't keep quiet about what really matters to them. If something's important, they stick up for themselves in a way that is respectful to others, but also lets those other people know that their actions were wrong.

Kendra

Kendra walked into the lunchroom. She saw her close friend Tanya sitting with a group of girls. Kendra started to walk to their table. Then one of the girls said loudly, "Oh no. Here comes Kendra." The girl also said something mean about Kendra's clothes and hair. All the girls laughed—even Tanya. Kendra was shocked and hurt that her friend laughed. She turned away, walked to another table, and sat down. She started to think of something nasty to say to those girls—especially Tanya.

Just then, Kendra remembered to "Stop, Think, Choose, and Think Again." She asked herself, "What should I do?"

At first, more mean ideas came into Kendra's mind. Maybe she could say nasty things to the girls before lunch was over. That might feel good for a minute. But then what would happen? They might pick on her more. Maybe she could get her brother and his friends to threaten the girls. That would scare them! But it would also get her brother and his friends in trouble. The girls might fight back. The students might end up in trouble with the principal. They'd want to get back at Kendra. And then Kendra would still have a problem—a bigger one.

Kendra thought, "I could just be quiet and try to forget about it." But then she thought again. Ignoring those girls was probably smart. But what about Tanya? Why had Tanya laughed? Was she trying to fit in with the popular girls? Or didn't she want to be friends anymore? Kendra did want to try to stay friends with Tanya because they had a good history together. But Kendra decided she couldn't ignore what Tanya did.

She wondered if she could try to talk to Tanya later, alone. She could ask her why she laughed. She could hear what Tanya had to say, and tell her that the laughing hurt. She could do this without yelling or being mean. This would be assertive. Both girls could try to sort things out and feel better.

They did talk. Tanya said she felt awful about how she acted. She had done it to be accepted by the other girls. Kendra and Tanya talked about ways to keep it from happening again.

Being assertive is smart. Assertive people have a better chance of getting what they want. That's because they say what they mean clearly and strongly, but they don't attack the other person. They solve the problem. Think about it: You don't win an argument when you "beat" someone by proving the person is wrong. That only makes the other person turn into an enemy. You win when you get the person to see things your way. In fact, then you

BOTH win. You both feel okay about things.

A Challenge for You

Read the challenge and look at choices 1, 2, and 3. Also read results A, B, and C. Match the letter for the result that would probably happen to the number of the choice. Write your answers on a piece of paper, or in your notebook. (When you're done, you can compare your choices to the in section entitled "Solutions to Some of the Challenges and Questions".)

CHALLENGE: For weeks, a bully has pushed Jake around. Finally, Jake shoves him back. The hallway monitor sees this. He scolds Jake and takes him to the principal's office. The principal gives Jake detention. Jake thinks that this punishment is unfair. Here are three ways Jake could react.

Which one is assertive and tries to solve the problem with respect?

1. Jake could yell at the principal. He could shout, "You should punish the hall monitor for catching the wrong kid!"

2. Jake could tell the principal why he pushed the other kid. Then he could ask, "Is there something the school can do to protect us from bullies? Could we start a 'no-bullying' program like they have at my cousin's school?"

3. Jake could lower his head, say nothing, and take the punishment.

Which is the most likely result of each choice?

A. Later, the bully laughs at Jake and threatens him. Every time Jake walks by the hallway monitor, he sternly reminds Jake to behave.

B. The principal gets upset and gives Jake more detention.

C. The principal says, "I'll look into it." Later, she calls the boy who was bullying into her office.

3. Say "I" Instead of "You"

People don't like to be told that they are doing wrong things. They don't like to hear "You're wrong!" or "You're being mean!" They hear that blaming word **"YOU."** Then they get angry, or angrier. This doesn't help make anything better.

Here's a way to be assertive when you talk, without criticizing or blaming: Tell how you feel by using the words **"I," "me,"** and **"my"** instead of "you."

Below are some things people say to others. The "you-talk" statements use the word "you." The "I-talk" statements use "I," "me," or "my." Which ones would you want somebody to say to you?

"You-Talk"

- "You aren't listening."
- "You're rude!"
- "You did a lousy job cleaning up."
- "You're not being fair."

"I-Talk"

- "I want what I'm saying to be listened to."
- "I don't like to be talked to that way."
- "I need to work at a clean table."
- "To me, that doesn't seem fair."

Can you see how I-talk avoids making others upset? That's because it doesn't blame someone for what's happening. It simply says how a situation affects the person who's talking. Using I-talk lets you be assertive. It lets you **speak up,** in a **strong but polite** way, without using a harsh voice or angry words.

A Challenge for You

Change the angry you-talk to I-talk. Write your answers on a piece of paper, or in your notebook. (When you're done, you can compare your choices to the solutions in section entitled "Solutions to Some of the Challenges and Questions".) Then practice saying the I-talk statements in a strong, polite tone of voice.

CHALLENGE 1: Hector tries to do his work, but doesn't know how. When he asks for help, his teacher says, "I already showed you this." At lunchtime, Hector isn't done. Mrs. Travis lets the other students go. But she says to Hector, "You'll be eating lunch with me today while you do the work." Hector yells out, "You witch! You're the one who ought to be doing the work. You know how and I don't! You're mean and you never help anybody."

CHALLENGE 2: Maggie's watch has a broken wristband. During a test, she puts the watch on her desk. She wants to keep track of how much time is left. She finishes early and leaves her desk to hand in her test. She asks for a pass to go to the bathroom. When she returns to her desk five minutes later, the watch is gone. Kevin is looking at her and smiling. Maggie yells out, "Mr. Tess, Kevin stole my watch!" Kevin says that he didn't do it. Maggie says, "Yes you did. I saw you smiling. You're a thief!"

CHALLENGE 3: Tim and Sasha are working on a project together. They have to write their report on the computer. Sasha starts writing the paper while Tim Notice when other people use goes to the library for a book they need. When he returns, he reads what Sasha wrote. He says,

"What are you doing? You're writing it all wrong. You're not supposed to start by telling what we think. First we have to write about all the other possible answers and why they were wrong. You're going to make us late handing in the project."

CHALLENGE 4: Mr. Cannon is mad at the class for acting up, and he takes away next week's field trip. Ira talks with the other students during lunch. He tells them that they have to stand up to Mr. C. When they return to class, Mr. C. tries to start the lesson. He tells the class to take out their science books. Ira says, "You're not getting any work from us until you give the field trip back. You can talk all you want, but you'll be talking to yourself." Mr. C. says he will give out punishments to students who don't get out their books. Most of the students get their books from their desks. Ira and a few others don't. They get detention.

IDEA!

Notice when other people use you-talk. In your notebook or journal, write down blaming statements that you hear people use. Change those statements to I-talk. Keep noticing you-talk and thinking about I-talk. This is a good way to get used to using I-talk naturally. If you do make a negative "you" statement, say, "Excuse me. What I meant to say was [say I-message here]."

Along with I-talk, you can also use the words **"we"** and **"us."** For example, you and your sister might ask your parent, "We'd really like to finish watching our program before we do the dishes. Would that be okay?" You and some other kids in class might say to your teacher, "We're hoping we can have more time during class to finish our project. Would that be okay?"

IT'S YOUR TURN

Practice being assertive with somebody. Have the person pretend to be someone who does something you don't like. Think of

> a way to stick up for yourself in a strong, polite way. Use I-talk, and be sure to use a respectful but firm tone of voice.

I-talk can be tricky to do at first, especially when you're upset with someone. Once you get the hang of it, it's easier. Keep in mind the number one rule of I-talk: Never, NEVER, **NEVER** use the word "you" unless it's in a positive way ("I like how you handled that situation.") or a neutral way ("What do you suggest?"). Always avoid using "you" in a negative way ("You're not doing it right!").

Sometimes, it's just natural to say "you." Sometimes, you might feel like you want to blame the other person. But how will that help you get what you want? The important thing is to solve a problem or avoid it, not make things worse. So instead of blaming, be assertive and use I-talk.

> ### REMEMBER...
>
> **You will really have to be strong to stay with your new and better choices. Things that happen in school and at home will challenge you. They can make you think about going back to the old ways of acting. Other kids will try to get you to make bad choices. Sometimes things won't seem fair. You may want to yell, or blame, or argue. Don't do it! Instead, ask yourself: "Is this a good choice? Is it going to help me become the person I want to be?" Stay assertive. Take charge of your behavior!**

CHAPTER 5

Ways to Help Yourself Make Good Choices in School

"I like to say funny things about the lesson when teachers are teaching. Usually the other kids laugh. Some teachers laugh, but others don't. It depends on the teacher. Knowing when it's okay to say funny things and when it's not isn't easy." —Malik, 14

Many kids who have behavior challenges don't like school (or some parts of it). After all, it's not fun or rewarding to be in a place where the teachers and kids get upset with you. But these things can change. You can learn "tricks" that have helped other kids with behavior challenges. This chapter tells about some of those tricks. They are ways to help you make better choices in class. If you use them, things will get better for you in school. Then you'll find that you like being there more of the time.

Be Prepared

When you get ready to go into your classroom, think about what behaviors you need to show in there to be a success. As you walk through the door, remind yourself to do them.

Reuben

Reuben enters the school building. On the way to school, he has been thinking about his goal for the day. Now he gives himself one more reminder. He hangs up his jacket and gets things out of his backpack. Then he starts to talk with one of his friends. The teacher tells everyone to sit down and listen to the announcements. Reuben goes to his seat and listens to the voice coming over the speaker. Next to the speaker is the list of class rules. He looks at them and sees that he is already doing two things right: The first rule is "Be ready to learn." Reuben is ready. He has his notebook and pencil out on the desk. The second rule is "Be quiet when the teacher is talking." The teacher on the speaker isn't his classroom teacher, but it's a teacher just the same. And Reuben is being quiet. He looks at the other class rules. He reminds himself to raise his hand if he wants to say something during class. If Reuben can keep following the rules, he'll have a good day at school, learn a lot, and earn his teacher's respect.

Did you notice that Reuben thought about how to act before he went into class? He also looked at the class rules before the lesson began. These are ways Reuben has learned to be prepared for school.

Patty

Patty gets scolded by the teacher for talking to a friend during the lesson. Geez! Patty was trying so hard to follow the rules, but she just forgot for a minute. She reminds herself of what she's supposed to do: Listen while the teacher is teaching. Patty says, "Oops. I'm sorry, Mr. Chen." She puts her eyes on him and listens to what he is saying.

IT'S YOUR TURN

- **Think about your usual classroom (or classes). Now think of the rules and expectations there. What behaviors should you remind yourself to use before you go into each room?**
- **Think about other classes and places at school. What rules do you need to remember for:**

    the halls?
    art class?
    lunch?
    the gym?
    assemblies?
    recess?

> the bathroom?
> homeroom?
> the drinking fountain?
> the bus?
> **Before you go from one place to another in school, think about the rules for the new place. Get yourself prepared to follow the rules.**

How could Patty have stayed out of trouble? Thinking about the rules she needed to follow would have helped her. But everyone makes mistakes sometimes. After her first mistake, Patty thought about the rules. In this way, she prepared herself to do better in the future.

Ask for Help from Others

You can ask other kids to stop you if they see you make a bad choice about behavior. This can be a good way to make your chances of success stronger. Just be sure to ask people you trust. And when they remind you, don't act mad at them. Remember that they're helping you do the right thing.

Just nod "yes" and then show the right behavior. Thank your helpers after class.

Jack

"Why do you keep doing that?" Jack's teacher said in an angry voice. "Stop it now." Jack took his pencil out of his mouth. He got caught chewing it again. It's so hard for him to stop.

At recess, Jack asked his friend Lakeesha to help him. Lakeesha was a good friend who sat behind Jack. Jack knew Lakeesha could see him bring the pencil up to his face. He said, "Hey Keesh. If you see me start to chew my pencil, can you poke me once so I stop? I gotta quit doing it."

"Sure," said Lakeesha.

Later that day, Jack started chewing his pencil. Lakeesha gave him a gentle poke, and he stopped. She stopped him another time later. After school, Jack thanked her.

IDEA!

Who can remind you to show the correct behaviors at school? Think of a good signal the person can use.

Maybe a classmate can look at you and pull on his ear or tap your arm. Tell your teacher about the signal, too. When teachers know what's going on, they won't get upset if someone gives you the signal.

Five "Tricks" to Help You Track Your Progress

Sometimes it helps to keep track of how you are doing at stopping a wrong behavior or choosing a better one. This chapter explains five "tricks" you can use to do this.

1. Keep a Goal Record

A goal record lets you see your progress on making good choices. Below pages has a "Goal Record" form that you can use. Here's how to use your form:

- **First, copy or print the form** at school (ask permission first!) or at the library. You can make two or three copies if you want to work on

more than one behavior. But working on one is a good start.
- **At the top** of the form, write your goal for the week. This is a behavior you'd like to show more often in class.
- **On the side** of the form, write the parts of your school day. These are places where you are located at different times—see the picture below.
- **Each day,** notice how you did in each time or place on the form. For each part of the day, give yourself a "grade" from 0 to 3. (3 is the best—it means you've met your goal.) You might have the teacher or a friend rate you, too. That will help you see if you are noticing your behavior accurately.

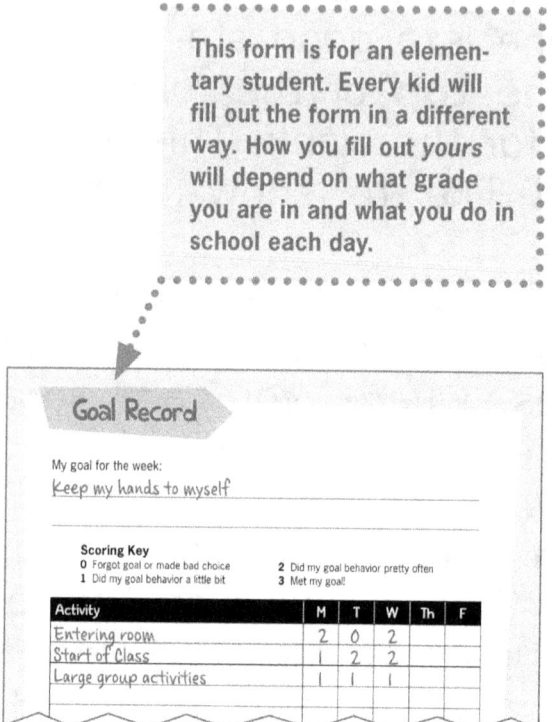

Carry your goal record around in your backpack, or keep it in your desk. Mark it each day for a week. At the end of the week, take a look at how you did. Congratulate yourself for good behavior choices. Then ask yourself how you're doing in the "big picture." Should you set a new goal that is harder to do? Should you practice the same goal again? Should you set an easier goal? Once you decide, start the next week using a new form.

You can make your own form if you want. It should include your weekly goal and space for tracking your behavior all during your school day. Your school or teacher might have a special goal record form, too.

2. Use Plus (+) and Minus (-)

Here's another trick to help you notice your behavior during the day. Think of something that could remind you to notice your behavior. This is your own personal signal. It could be anything that happens at least a few times during a class. It might be a clock tick. (You don't have to hear every one, just a few.) It could be someone saying the teacher's name. It could be hearing someone going by in the hallway. It could be the bell or the sound of the pencil sharpener. It could be anytime someone raises a hand to speak or whenever someone enters the room. Also have a sheet of paper ready. The paper should be just for noticing behavior.

Whenever you hear or see your signal, think about your behavior **right at that moment.** If you were doing the right thing in the classroom, write a plus (+) sign. If you were making a wrong choice, write a minus (-) sign. (You don't have to notice every one of the signals. But when you do become aware of the signal, check your behavior right then.)

At the end of the day, count the plus and minus signs. Every day, try to have **MORE** plus signs and **FEWER** minus signs than you did the day before.

3. Beat Your Previous Best

Bad habits can be hard to stop. We are so used to doing them! They become almost automatic. Sometimes it's best to try to break habits a little bit at a time. One way to do this is with a system for making small improvements. Make a copy of or print out the "Beat Your Previous Best" form. Cut out one card. (Save the rest to use later.) Think of a wrong behavior choice that can be counted. (Examples are using curse words, insulting someone, complaining about the work, or saying an answer without being called on.)

Keep your card with you. Check off a box each time you show that bad behavior choice. For behaviors you do a lot, look at the card at the end of the class period. (For example, look at it when science or math is over for the day.) For behaviors you don't do as often, look at the card at the end of the day. Count how many times you showed the wrong behavior. Now set a goal: Do the behavior one less time during the next class period or day. Repeat this the next period or next day.

When you meet your new goal, set a new one of again doing it one less time.

Bit by bit, the behavior will disappear. In the meantime, take pride in your progress and improvement.

> ### Try This Fun Exercise!
>
> Are habits hard to break? You bet. Impossible? No way! It's difficult to change, but you can do it. This exercise will prove it:
>
> **1.** Cross your arms over your chest.
>
> **2.** Look at your hands. Which hand is on top of the other arm?
>
> **3.** Which hand is tucked under?
>
> **4.** Uncross your arms and cross them again ... but this time, **switch** the way you place your hands.
>
> **5.** Keep switching back and forth between the two ways until you can do it without having to think about it very much!

4. Set and Reach Small Goals

Some people think that it is better to give attention to **positive** behavior, not bad choices. (For example, the "Beat Your Previous Best" exercise puts the focus on a problem behavior.) To help students pay attention to positive behavior, there is something called **shaping.** It lets them reach a big behavior goal by breaking it down into little goals. With shaping, you set small goals. Each time you meet a small goal, you set another small goal. Each small goal gets you closer to the bigger behavior goal. The small goals add up. Soon, they lead you to reaching the big goal that you wanted to accomplish. You build better behavior one small improvement at a time.

Here are the steps you can follow to make a **shaping plan.** You can copy the "Shaping Plan" form and use that if you want. Do these on your own or with help from a teacher, family grown-up, or friend:

1. **Set a big goal.** Set your goal for a smart behavior choice you want to make in the future. Ask yourself, "What behavior do I want to show in class?" This is your big goal. Write it down. Write down the **GOOD** behavior you **WANT** to show.
2. **Look at how you're doing right now.** Ask yourself, "How am I doing on meeting that goal right now?" Describe the problem behavior that you are showing now. Write down this behavior that you want to get rid of. Then move to the small goals.
3. **Set a small goal.** Look at what you wrote for "How I'm Doing Now." Think of a small thing you can do that is a **little bit** better than how you are doing right now. This is your first small goal. Write it down. Be sure it says what you **WILL** do in class or at home (*not* what you *won't* do). It doesn't have to be a big change—just a small improvement.
4. **Set other small goals.** Think of another little goal. This goal should

be harder to do than the first small goal. Write it down. Keep writing other small goals. Each one should be slightly harder than the one before it. Each goal should get you closer to the big goal you wrote.

5. **Start trying to meet the first small goal.** At the start of the day, look at your first small goal. Work to meet that goal today.

6. **See how you did.** At the end of the day, think about how you did. Did you meet the small goal? Congratulate yourself! Then decide if you should try the same one again tomorrow, or try to meet the next small goal on your list. If you didn't meet the goal, think about it again. Ask yourself, "Should I try for the same goal again tomorrow? Or should I think of a smaller goal?"

7. **Choose your next small goal.** Maybe you'll try for the first small goal again. Maybe you'll go on to the next small goal. What if you think you need a smaller goal? Try to think of one that is easier to do but will still make you work a little.

8. **Keep working on the small goals.** Work on them one at a time. Each time you feel ready, move to the next step.

It's a good idea to get your teacher's approval to do things this way. Most teachers will be happy to help you with your plan. They would like to see you improve.

Here is an example of a shaping plan:

Shaping Plan

Big Goal: Finish and hand in my math homework.

How I'm Doing Now: I don't finish my math homework, so I don't turn it in.

Small Goal 1: Hand in the homework sheet with my name and date at the top.
Small Goal 2: Do Small Goal 1 AND do one of the math homework problems.
Small Goal 3: Do Small Goal 1 AND five of the problems.
Small Goal 4: Do Small Goal 1 AND all the even-numbered problems.
Small Goal 5: Do Small Goal 1 and ALL the problems except for one.
Small Goal 6: Do Small Goal 1 AND all the problems
Small Goal 7: Keep doing Small Goal 6 for 2 weeks.

5. Make a Contract with Your Teacher

You've probably heard of contracts before. They are written agreements between people. Sports players have contracts. They get paid a certain amount of money to play for a team. Music groups and singers have contracts. They agree to perform at a certain time and place. Then they'll get a certain amount of money.

Kids can set up contracts with teachers to get a reward for doing something in school. (Rewards at school probably won't be money!) The kids get the reward if they do what they agreed to do. (Kids can also have contracts at home with parents.) If you would like to make a contract, you'll have to make a deal by bargaining with the teacher. You'll promise to do something the teacher wants you to do. For example, your teacher might want you to be on time for class. The teacher will promise to give you a reward (maybe points toward a privilege or prize) when you do *exactly* what you agree to do in your contract.

Here are the steps to follow to make a contract:
1. Set up a meeting with the teacher.
2. Have the teacher tell you what behavior she or he would like to see you do. Or suggest your own idea for a behavior to your teacher.
3. Tell the teacher what reward you would like to have. It could be a class duty. It could be more time on the computer. It could be a free lunch, a baseball cap ... whatever. You might want to have a list of rewards ready, in case the teacher doesn't agree to some of your first ideas.
4. With the teacher, talk about how much you have to do to get a certain reward. Figure it out together. Make a deal.

IT'S YOUR TURN

• **Think of a behavior you want to work on changing in school. Which of the ideas in this chapter**

> might help you change to a better behavior?
> • Talk with your teacher about what way could work best for you. You might even do two ways at once. For example, maybe you'll do a shaping plan. Then you could use plus and minus to help you reach the goals.

5. Write down your agreement. This is your contract. Be very exact about **how much** you must do and **when** you will do it. Also write:
   • exactly what the reward will be
   • who will decide that you have done what the contract says you will do
   • a date when the two of you will meet again to see how the contract is working (so you can rewrite the contract if something isn't fair)
   • a place to sign and date the contract
6. Now it's time for you and the teacher to sign the contract. You

might want to get a witness to sign it, too. The witness will help decide if you and the adult are being fair and obeying the rules in the contract.

You will find a contract form in below pages. You can photocopy or print out the form to use if you want. Your teacher might have a different contract form, too. Or the two of you could make one together.

REMEMBER...

School will be a much nicer place to be if you can choose to show good behavior. It helps to have a few different "tricks" for doing this. Give the ideas in this chapter a try. See which ones work best for you. As you get used to using the ideas, you will make progress. You will start to make better behavior choices more often. Then you'll learn more, enjoy class more, and get along better with teachers and with other students. Chapter 6 has more tips for getting along better

> **with your teachers (and other people).**

From *The Survival Guide for Kids with Behavior Challenges* by Tom McIntyre, Ph.D., copyright © 2013. Free Spirit Publishing Inc., Minneapolis, MN; 800-735-7323; www.freespirit.com. This page may be reproduced for individual, classroom, or small group work only. For other uses, contact www.freespirit.com/company/permissions.cfm.

Goal Record

My goal for the week:

[Space left intentionally blank in original book]

Scoring Key
0 Forgot goal or made bad choice
1 Did my goal behavior a little bit
2 Did my goal behavior pretty often
3 Met my goal!

Activity	M	T	W	Th	F

Beat Your Previous Best

To learn how to use these cards to beat your previous best,.

From *The Survival Guide for Kids with Behavior Challenges* by Tom McIntyre, Ph.D., copyright © 2013. Free Spirit Publishing Inc., Minneapolis, MN; 800-735-7323; www.freespirit.com. This page may be reproduced for individual, classroom, or small group work only.

For other uses, contact www.freespirit.com/company/permissions.cfm.

Shaping Plan

Big Goal: _____
[Space left intentionally blank in original book]

How I'm Doing Now: _____
[Space left intentionally blank in original book]

Small Goal 1: _____
Small Goal 2: _____
Small Goal 3: _____
Small Goal 4: _____
Small Goal 5: _____
Small Goal 6: _____
Small Goal 7: _____
Small Goal 8: _____
Small Goal 9: _____
Small Goal 10: _____

You might not have 10 small goals. Just use the spaces you need. If you have more small goals, add them on the back or use another copy of the form.

From *The Survival Guide for Kids with Behavior Challenges* by Tom McIntyre, Ph.D., copyright © 2013. Free

Spirit Publishing Inc., Minneapolis, MN; 800-735-7323; www.freespirit.com. This page may be reproduced for individual, classroom, or small group work only. For other uses, contact www.freespirit.com/company/permissions.cfm.

Contract

This is an agreement between _____ and
(student)

_____.
(teacher)

Agreement

The student will do this: _____

[Space left intentionally blank in original book]

If the student does what is written, the teacher will do this:

[Space left intentionally blank in original book]

Conditions of Agreement

1: _____
2: _____
3: _____
4: _____

This contract is in effect as soon as it is signed. The teacher and student will review it on _____.
(day/date)

Signatures

Student: _____
Teacher: _____
Witness: _____
Date: _____

From *The Survival Guide for Kids with Behavior Challenges* by Tom McIntyre, Ph.D., copyright © 2013. Free Spirit Publishing Inc., Minneapolis, MN; 800-735-7323; www.freespirit.com. This page may be reproduced for individual, classroom, or small group work only. For other uses, contact www.freespirit.com/company/permissions.cfm.

CHAPTER 6

Ways to Get Along Better with Teachers

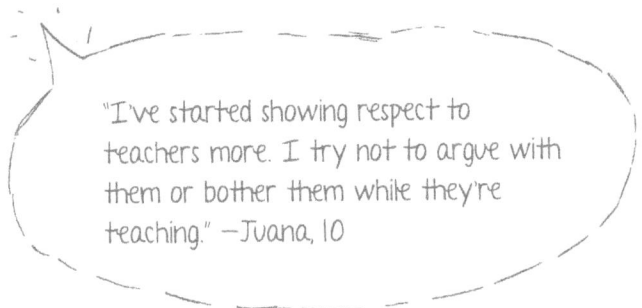

"I've started showing respect to teachers more. I try not to argue with them or bother them while they're teaching." —Juana, 10

Did you know that you **(yes, YOU)** can help teachers be nicer to you? It's true. You can do things to help teachers treat you better. This chapter gives you some ways to do this.

Say Nice Things to Teachers

Make teachers notice you at times when they're not busy or upset. Then they get to say something positive to you. Say hello in a clear, pleasant voice. Put a smile on your face, too. Add the teacher's title and name ("Mrs.

Mufti," "Mr. Tate"). This gives your greeting a personal touch. It also gives teachers the respect they like.

Once you're comfortable saying hello, add comments and compliments. Say something nice about the teacher's class. You can even compliment the teacher's clothes. Or you can remark on something the teacher has done. This is a great way to help teachers see you in a "better light."

"Hey, Mr. McGee. How are you doing today? It was fun to do that experiment yesterday. Are we doing another one tomorrow?"

"That was a great speaker you got for career day, Ms. Silmon."

"Mrs. Marco, I did just what you said would work. And it did. That was good advice."

"Nice tie, Mr. B."

People like to hear nice things about themselves. They usually like the people who say these things. Don't you? So give teachers compliments. Then they will probably start to be nicer to you.

> **Try to only say nice things that you really mean. Most people can tell when a compliment is fake. The teacher needs to feel that you mean what you say if you want to get the results you seek.**

Let Teachers Teach

One of the main reasons kids get in trouble is because they keep teachers from teaching. It makes sense to follow the rules that allow teaching and learning to happen, and avoid arguing with teachers. Let's face it. Teachers have a lot of power. They can give kids lots of punishments (and rewards!). Plus, if you have an **IEP team** (you can learn more about this in Chapter 13), they will ask your teachers if you are improving making good choices. You want your teachers to tell the team good news. So let teachers teach. **That's their job.** That's what they're paid to do. And not only that: Teachers became teachers because they like kids and want them to learn important things. Some of these things might be ones that you don't realize yet will be important in your life.

IT'S YOUR TURN

• **Pick a teacher you don't know well or have had problems with. Say hi and notice the result. Even if nothing changes after one hello, don't give up. Try saying it every day for three days, or even for a week. See what happens.**

• **Think of a teacher who you would like to treat you better. (It might be the one you've been saying hi to.) Make a plan. Think of what comments and compliments you'll say. When will you say them? Practice with someone first. That way you'll feel more confident when you say them to your teacher. Keep at it.**

> **See what happens after a few days.**

Really listen if teachers stop the lesson to tell you something. They are trying to let you know what is the right thing to do right now. Some teachers do this in a friendly way. Others don't always say it very nicely. In that case, ignore the unfriendly tone and listen to the meaning of their words. Even if the way something is said sounds negative, focus on understanding the message behind the tone: Teachers want you and others to be able to learn important things.

But what if you have a good point? What if you think that the teacher should listen to you right now, even though you've been asked to focus on something else? What if you really want to say something right now, even though you've been told to stop? Later, if your concern still seems important, you can ask the teacher for a moment to talk with you. Save what you have to say until the lesson is over, and, if you still think the teacher is wrong, speak with him or her about it in private. You could wait until free time, or recess, or lunchtime, or after class. But for right now, just say "Okay" and follow the directions. It's important to be assertive, but you also have to know when to be that way. Being assertive when a teacher is trying to teach and others are trying to learn is the wrong time. Instead, be respectfully assertive when the teacher has the time to listen to you.

When you do talk, speak politely. Don't argue. (Arguing won't get you what you want.) Instead, try using a question or making a request with a "sandwich." These are the next two things you'll read about in this chapter.

Make Suggestions with Questions

Suppose you don't like an assignment the teacher gave you. Refusing to do it will **NOT** help. It also won't help to say **negative** things, like "This stinks" or "This is stupid." And it definitely won't help to say rude things, like "I'm not doing this stuff" or "Do it yourself!" These are sure ways to get in trouble.

Instead, be **assertive:** Use a strong, polite voice to say what's on your mind. Use the word "I" instead of "you." (This is called I-talk, remember? You can read more about it in section entitled "3. Say "I" Instead of "You"".) Then suggest another way of doing things. How? By asking a question. No one likes to be bossed around. That's why it's important to ask, not demand.

IDEA!

Think of a teacher who sometimes gets upset about your behavior. Make a deal with yourself to say "Okay" to everything this teacher tells you to do tomorrow. After class, think about how you did. Did your behavior prevent trouble? If so, make the same choice again tomorrow.

Luci

Mr. Rivera told Luci, "Please read aloud starting at below pages." Luci had problems reading. She wanted to think of an excuse so she didn't have to read, but she tried to read it, and stumbled through. The other kids giggled and whispered. Luci was really embarrassed, especially when the teacher stopped her. He said, "That's enough, Luci. Bob, please read that part again." Luci felt foolish—and mad. But even though it was hard, she kept quiet.

After class, Luci went to the teacher. She said to him, "Mr. Rivera, I have problems with reading. I'm getting extra help to improve my skills. Could you tell me the day before which parts I'm going to read out loud? I'll practice it at home so I read it well the next day."

Mr. Rivera thought Luci had a good idea. He agreed to tell her ahead of time. He showed her a part to prepare for the next day.

Luci was embarrassed and upset in class. But she still made good choices. She waited for the right time to talk to the teacher. When they talked, she was assertive. She made a suggestion by asking a question. As a result, she got the help that she needed. And her teacher saw that Luci was able to work politely with him.

Like Luci, you can ask (not tell) about what you want. You can give a reason why it would be a good idea. Here are two examples of ways to try to get help. They show the difference between telling and asking.

"I'd learn more if I did it on the computer."

This is a way of telling, not asking. It sounds bossy. Teachers don't like to be told how to teach.

"Ms. Cobb, would it be okay to do it on the computer? That way I can add diagrams and show my ideas better."

IT'S YOUR TURN

Turn these orders into questions:
- **"Let me do the project with Tony."**
- **"It would work better to use paint instead of colored pencils."**
- **"Give me the sharper scissors so I can cut this out."**

This time the student gives a suggestion in the form of a question. She gives the reason for asking the question, too. Plus, she uses the teacher's title ("Ms.") and name ("Cobb"). Teachers like this. It shows respect.

When you make suggestions with questions, you won't always get your way. But you'll have a better chance of getting what you want.

Make a "Sandwich"

Got a gripe that's so important you can't just say "Okay" right now? If so, put it between two nice comments.
1. Start off by saying something that will please the teacher. It could be a nice comment about the class. Or it could be a compliment about how the teacher teaches.
2. Next, tell what the problem is. Try not to make it a bossy or whiny complaint. Instead, say the important thing you want in a way that's assertive. You can even make a suggestion with a question when you do this. The main thing is to be friendly and show respect.
3. Finish quickly with another nice remark. It can be the same nice thing as before, or something new. It might be another compliment. It might let the teacher know how you have been helped. It might be a thank you.

Think of these three steps as making a request sandwich. The nice things are the two pieces of bread. The important thing you want (your request) is the peanut butter or cheese that goes in the middle.

Here are the three parts of a request sandwich:

SOMETHING NICE "That was a good explanation about subtracting fractions, Ms. Clinton. Seeing the parts of the whole objects helped."

WHAT YOU WANT "Could you please explain how to do percents by showing drawings of the parts like that, too?"

SOMETHING ELSE NICE "You did a great job of helping us understand how to take fractions away from fractions."

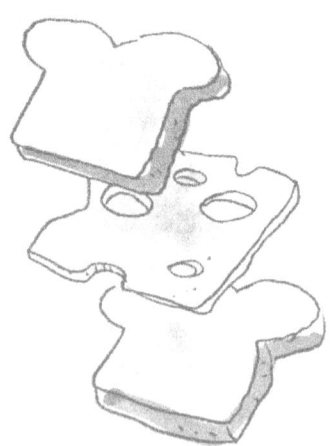

Here's the whole sandwich, put together:

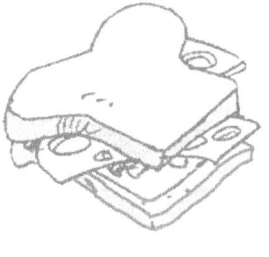

"That was a good explanation about subtracting fractions, Ms. Clinton. Seeing the parts of the whole objects helped. Could you please explain how to do percents by showing drawings of the parts like that, too? You did a great job of helping us understand how to take fractions away from fractions."

Here are three different ways students talk to teachers. In each case, the student has something important to say or ask. Which is a sandwich?

"This is stupid. We did this last year. Why do we have to do this stuff again?"

You probably figured out that this isn't the sandwich. It doesn't start with something nice. In fact, there's nothing nice anywhere.

"I think it would be better if we did it like we did last year. That was fun. It isn't going to be any fun this way."

This says that last year was fun. But it doesn't start with a compliment. And it ends with a complaint. It's not the kind of thing a teacher will be glad to hear.

> "The way you explained it made it really easy, Mr. Hill. It reminded me of what we learned last year. I was wondering: If we can prove that we know this stuff, could we learn something else instead? That would be great, 'cause the way you teach new stuff makes it interesting."

This starts with a compliment: It tells the teacher he helped the student learn. The message in the middle is friendly, and it doesn't sound like complaining. But it tells the teacher what the student wants. Then it ends with another compliment. What teacher wouldn't like to hear this?

A Challenge for You

This is a challenge in two parts. Do it in your notebook, one part at a time. (When you're done, you can compare your ideas to the solutions in section entitled "Solutions to Some of the Challenges and Questions".)

CHALLENGE 1: Here are the three parts of a request sandwich. Put them in the right order.

"But I think a zero grade is unfair. I couldn't do the paper last night because I left my notebook at Paula's. Could I please turn it in after lunch? That's when I'll see her and get my notebook back."

"Miss Lange, I agree with you that it is important to do my schoolwork."

"I really enjoyed doing the report on Ben Franklin, and learned a lot. I think you'll like the paper if you take it late."

CHALLENGE 2: Aron is known for being late to class a lot. His goal this week is to get to class on time. He enters the door to class as the bell is ringing. He thinks that he is on time. Mr. Hunter says, "You're late. Go to the office and get a late pass." Aron gives a surprised look. Mr. Hunter says, "You have to be in your seat when the bell rings. Go to the office." Aron doesn't want to miss any of the class. And he will miss a lot if he goes to the office. He wants to explain

> this to Mr. Hunter. Write a request sandwich for Aron.

Use "Behavior Mod"

Have you ever heard of **behavior modification?** It is a scientific way of changing the way people act. Sometimes it's called **behavior mod.**

Some scientists study why people do what they do. They found out that if people get a reward for doing something, they show more of that behavior. The reward makes them want to do it again. It's nice to get a reward (like a thank you, a prize, or a smile).

When teachers reward you for good behavior, they're using behavior mod. They're helping you change (modify) your behavior. You can even use this on yourself. In Chapter 5, you learned tricks for tracking your progress in changing behavior. These are ways to use behavior mod.

And guess what? You can use behavior mod with teachers, too. Yes, really! You can decide on a behavior you'd like your teacher to use with you.

You can "reward" the teacher for using it.

Think of all the things students can do that are rewarding to teachers. They can pay attention. They can do their assignments. They can say "Okay." They can ask good questions about the lesson. They can say nice things about the class. They can follow rules and directions.

"Reward" your teacher. So how do you help teachers be nicer and more helpful to you? Reward them when they do things you like! This doesn't mean giving teachers prizes. It means letting them know when **their** teaching is helping **you** learn. For example:
- When your teacher teaches an interesting lesson, nod your head and pay attention.
- When a teacher speaks nicely to you, smile and be nice, too.
- Maybe your teacher gives you fun projects or lets you do interesting computer activities. Tell the teacher how much you enjoy doing those things.
- Maybe the teacher explains things well. Say, "Thanks. Now I get it."

- Some teachers like to tell jokes. If yours does, smile or chuckle.

These are all ways to reward the behavior you like. Then you'll probably see more of that behavior in the future.

Help your teacher do nice things. Sometimes you'll have to help teachers do the nice things in the first place. Then you can reward that behavior when they show it. For example, you can ask for help in a polite way:

"Mr. Smith, I did the first two questions. How does it look so far?"

"I think I'm finished. Is this how you wanted it?"

It's probably best to ask these types of questions only two or three times during a class. (Any more might annoy the teacher.) And it's even better when you mention something from the lesson before you ask for the help.

Mark

During math, Mark was having some problems when he tried to regroup numbers. He raised his hand to call the teacher over. Mark said, "Mrs. Petty, I remember that you said to borrow from the tens column. But can I borrow more than one ten?"

Mark showed Mrs. Petty that he was listening. He did this first, before he asked the question. (Teachers like that.) Mrs. Petty nodded and said, "I'm glad to know you listened, Mark. You may need to borrow from the tens column. You can't borrow more than one ten, though." Mark was happy he got this nice response from Mrs. Petty. He smiled at her and said, "Okay, I get it. Thanks."

If you try Mark's approach, remember to get attention in the right way. Raise your hand and wait. Don't get out of your seat or interrupt a teacher who's working with other kids. Wait until he or she is done. Then, when you have the teacher's attention, use a strong and polite voice.

5 Steps to Using Behavior Mod with a Teacher

1. Choose a teacher who you would like to see be nicer or more helpful to you.

2. Think about a behavior you want the teacher to do more often.

3. Figure out what you'll do to encourage the behavior. Maybe you'll reward it each time it happens. Or maybe you'll first find ways to help the teacher do nice things. Get some other students involved, too!

4. Think of rewards the teacher will like. You might use compliments, smiles, saying "Okay," or other things. You can use a different nice thing each time the behavior happens.

5. Try out your plan. Give it time to work. Notice ways of helping and which rewards work best.

Use Your Skills Together

In this chapter and earlier ones, you've learned lots of ways to get along better at school. You found out how important it is to build your self-esteem. You practiced how to "Stop, Think, Choose, and Think Again." You learned about being assertive and using I-talk. You read that it's important to be prepared and ask for help when you need it. You learned ways that will help you change your behavior and help your teachers want to treat you nicely.

IMPORTANT!

What if you have a teacher who treats you badly? What if there's a teacher who is NEVER nice or fair no matter what you do? Or one who says mean things, or just won't help you? Talk about this with a teacher you trust. Or talk to the school counselor. If you don't find help at school, talk to your parent, guardian, or another adult. Keep looking until you find an adult who can help you with this problem. Also ask an adult if you need help learning skills for getting along with teachers. (For a list of adults to talk to, see "Adults You Might Talk To".)

Often the information and skills you are learning can work together. As you get used to using each idea, you'll find that you do some things without having to think too hard first. You will also find that you are using the skills together to help yourself. That's how it is for Nina:

Nina

Nina gets a stern warning from Miss Tan for talking to Will. Nina was just doing something funny with the pencil that Will lent to her. She was going to get right back to work. She doesn't like how the teacher spoke to her. It sounded mean. Nina wants to say something mean back to the teacher.

She stops herself and remembers the goal she set for herself that morning: Say "Okay" to whatever the teacher says. So Nina says "Okay." But she can't stop thinking that Miss Tan treated her badly. Nina keeps imagining things she could have said back. She feels angry, like things aren't fair.

Nina doesn't like these feelings. They make her want to explode. She remembers the self-talk that she is practicing with the school counselor. She thinks to herself: "Stop! Cool down. Think. If I say those things, I'll get in trouble. But I want to let Miss Tan know how I feel about this."

Nina thinks about what she can do. Finally, a good idea comes to mind. "I know! I'll talk with Miss Tan when I'm leaving class. I'll tell her that I didn't like the way she spoke to me. I'd better be careful, though. I want her to treat me better. So I've got to show respect when I say what's on my mind."

Nina thinks some more and plans what she will say. She decides to say: "Miss Tan, I apologize for goofing around when I was getting a pencil. I like your class and I was going to get right to work. I'll try not to do that again. But if I make a mistake, could you just call my name next time? I promise to figure out what I'm supposed to be doing. Then I'll do it right away because I like what we're learning here."

After class, Nina says the words she planned. Miss Tan looks a little surprised. She says, "I'll think about it, but you have to remember to behave, right?" That's not quite what Nina wanted to hear. But she says "Okay." (That's her goal, remember?) She's pretty sure Miss Tan is thinking about doing something different next time. That's all that Nina really wants. Even if the teacher won't admit it, Nina has made a difference. She did it in a strong, positive way. She kept out of trouble, *and* she made things better by saying positive and respectful things to the teacher.

A Challenge for You

Think of the ideas you have learned in this book so far. Which of

> those ideas did Nina use? List them in your notebook. You may want to read the story again, making your list as you read. When you're done, compare your list to the in section entitled "Solutions to Some of the Challenges and Questions".

Many teachers are already nice to kids. Treat these teachers well, too. Be friendly and helpful. Cooperate in their classes. Reward their nice behavior that makes school a better place for you. Then they'll know you appreciate them. That way, they'll keep being nice.

It's usually easy to show this kind of respect to teachers who treat you well. It can be harder to show it to the ones who don't. For those teachers who seem not-so-nice, look for times when they **do** treat you well. (They probably do this once in a while.) Smile and do what they ask. Tell them how it makes you want to work hard in their classes. With time, they will probably start to treat you better more often.

Even if they don't, keep trying. And keep working to make good behavior choices yourself. You won't always have the teachers you have today. But you will always be you. **YOU** are the person who wants to feel better and have a better life. That means you need to take charge of your behavior.

> REMEMBER…
>
> **It's good to know ways to help your teachers help you. This can make a big difference in how you get along at school. But don't forget, the best way to change how teachers treat you is by changing your own behavior. When you make good choices, you and your teachers will get along better. You'll want to work harder for them, and they' re likely to treat you nicer, too!**

CHAPTER 7

Ways to Make and Keep Friends

"I wish I had better friends. I want friends who act right and help me stay out of trouble." —Jerome, 13

We all want people to like us. We want friends we can trust. Having good friends makes life at school and home more fun. But for many kids who have behavior challenges, it's not easy to make friends. Other kids don't always want to be friends. They don't like the behaviors and choices they often see kids with behavior challenges make. You're working on making better choices. If you keep at it, this shouldn't be a problem much longer. But sometimes kids who have behavior challenges haven't learned the ways to make and keep good friends. This chapter has tips for being friendly so that others will want to be your friend. It also has ideas for finding friends who are right for you.

Say Nice Things to Others

When you notice things you like about other people, say something nice. Look for chances to give compliments or say thank you. Depending on what is happening, you might say things like:

> "That was a good answer."
> "Your project really looks great."
> "That joke you made was funny."
> "Thanks for lending me a pen."
> "I like your jacket."

Why say nice things? Because people like to hear good things about themselves. Don't you? When you first try this, others may not be nice back to you. They need to know you truly mean well. They probably aren't used to hearing you say these things. They may remember when you teased them or made mean remarks. (No one likes that.) You have to show them a "new you," and keep showing it. Don't give up! In time, they'll see that you want to be a real friend.

Ask People About Themselves

When you're around other kids, **ask them questions** to get them talking. (Do this with adults, too.) You can ask them what they like to do for fun. Ask them which teams, bands, books, hobbies, or TV shows they enjoy. When they start to tell you about what they like, **listen closely.** Then you can ask them more questions about what they said. You can tell them what **YOU** think, too—in a friendly way. Try to keep the conversation going. There are lots of ways to do this. You might ask them why they like doing those things. Or ask how they got interested in them. A conversation involves both people. Be sure that both of you have a chance to say things back and forth.

Sometimes it can seem hard just to start a conversation with a kid at school. One idea is to try it first with people you know. Pick someone who will probably be friendly back to you. For example, you could ask a neighbor about himself. You could ask a relative. This could be someone your own age, or younger, or older.

IDEA!

Ask your counselor or special ed teacher about taking **social skills** lessons. These lessons let kids practice how to get along better with others. Social skills will help you make and keep friends. Section entitled "What About Resources for Grown-Ups?" tells where schools can find lessons to use.

Jody

Jody never knew what to say to relatives when they came over. One morning she found out that her uncle was coming to visit. Jody wondered how to get a conversation going. She thought about what her uncle liked to do. She knew one thing: He liked to fish. Jody thought of some questions to ask about that. She remembered that she had heard an ad for fishing gear on the radio. That gave her some ideas about questions she could ask.

After saying hello, Jody asked her uncle, "How's fishing?" Her uncle said, "Pretty good."

Jody thought of one of the questions she'd planned. "How do you know what time of day to fish?" she asked. Her uncle said it depended. The fish he liked to catch usually bit early in the morning.

Hearing that, Jody thought of another question: "What kind of fish do you like to go after?" Jody's uncle said he liked to fish for bass. That let Jody ask how her uncle knew what bait or lures to use. They talked for half an hour. Jody's uncle invited her on a fishing trip. After hearing so much about fishing, she thought that sounded fun.

What can talking to adult relatives have to do with making friends? Lots. Friends come from many places. You may want to make friends your own age at school. But don't forget that neighbors and relatives can be friends, too. People of different ages can be friends—or at least friendly! Like Jody, you might find that you can have fun with people you didn't know you would enjoy. Also like Jody, you can try out conversation skills with people you already know.

IT'S YOUR TURN

- **Are there some people you would like to talk with? Think of things they enjoy.**
- **Think of some questions you could ask them about what they like to do.**
- **If you know what they like, try to learn a little bit about it before you see them. You could find information in a magazine or**

library book. You could look on the Internet.

Give a Helping Hand

Chapter 2 talks about how starting a "helping habit" can build your self-esteem. Helping others is also a way to make friends. Remember a time when you had a big job to do and someone helped you out? Remember how it made the job easier? It was nice of that person, wasn't it? Helpful people are liked by others. Be helpful to everyone you **like** and **respect** (or think you want to get to know). Offer to help others when it looks like they could use a hand. Assist them when they are busy. Volunteer to share a chore.

Also tell teachers that you'd like to help with events they are planning. Maybe there's going to be a school dance. Maybe the class is doing a play or music program. If you offer to help get ready for these things, you'll get to work with other kids. This can be a good way to get to know new people and show that you want to make friends. You will have things in common. You'll have a chance to talk about those things.

Another idea for getting to know others is to become an expert in something. An expert knows a lot about a certain thing. If you know things that other kids like to talk and learn about, they'll come to you for help and advice. What would you like to become an expert about? Comics? A certain type of music? Pet care? Sports rules or facts? Once you decide on a topic, find books and videos or DVDs in the library, visit websites about that subject, find someone who knows more about it than you (and use your friendship communication skills), or team up with someone who wants to learn about the same things.

You want others to see the changes you are making. Helping out can be a good way to show people at school that you are changing your behavior. You can show this to people in your neighborhood, too.

IDEA!

Think of some younger kids who live in your neighborhood. Become their **mentor:** Ask their parents if you can help them out with their schoolwork (with their dad or mom nearby). If you see these kids around the neighborhood, say hello. Help them learn to do good things that you know how to do. Show them how to be a friend. Remember to be patient and kind with the children. Be sure to teach them how to make smart choices. One of the best ways to practice the new ways you're learning is to teach them to others.

Dantrell

Dantrell wanted to make friends with kids who lived near him. But there was a problem. Dantrell had behavior challenges. He was known for getting into trouble. Some parents didn't want him to play with their kids. Dantrell felt awful about this. He was working hard to make better choices. His teacher suggested that he try helping out some of the parents. That way, they would see that Dantrell was really changing his behavior.

Dantrell started offering to carry in groceries. He opened doors for people when they went in and out. He picked up things for people if they dropped them. He said hello to people and used his conversation skills. Word about "the new Dantrell" started to spread around the neighborhood. A couple of the parents started being nicer to him. After a while, they let him come over and play with their kids.

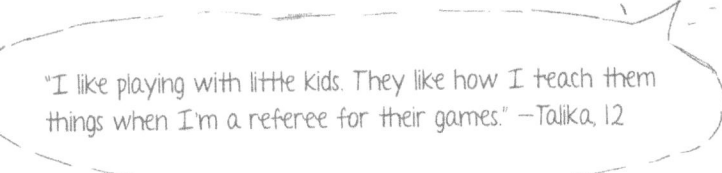

"I like playing with little kids. They like how I teach them things when I'm a referee for their games." —Talika, 12

Take Part in Activities

A great place to find new friends is in an after-school club or other organized group. There you can get to know others **outside of class.** You'll meet kids who like to do the same things you do. People who share the same interests often make good friends.

What if you're not sure how to join something? Or how to find a group?

First, think about what you want to do. This will help you figure out what to look for.

- What would you like to **know more** about? The way computers work? How to become a cheerleader? The secrets of great coaches? Why airplanes fly?

- What would you like to **learn** to do? Fish? Skate? Knit or sew? Cook? Turn cartwheels?
- What do you wish you could do **with someone else?** Take care of animals? Ride bikes? Write a TV script or a song?
- What sounds **fun?** Playing games? Doing stuff with little kids? Talking about books or movies? Planning a school event?

Then think of what groups you know about. These might be at your school. They might be activities in your community that you've seen or heard about. You might already go to a youth center, park, or place of worship. Often these are places where there are things going on.

Look for an activity that you would like. Look on bulletin boards at school and in your community. Check out the school yearbook. Look in your local newspaper. You can also find information online. Most schools, towns, cities, and counties have websites. These sites tell about clubs, lessons, sports, and other things people can do. If you don't have a computer at home, your school or library probably has one you can use. Also talk to students, teachers, and other kids and adults. Ask for their suggestions.

> ### IT'S YOUR TURN
> **Think about an activity you could do to meet people and make friends. If you want, use your notebook to list ideas and make plans. Decide on an activity. Then find out what you need to know in order to join in. Most groups don't require you to have special skills. They just want interested people.**

Visit the group or find out how to join in. Ask someone you know to help you find an activity. Be brave and give it a try!

> ### Activities for Making Friends
> **Sports (School or Community)**
> baseball or softball
> basketball
> in-line skating or skateboarding
> soccer

football
track or cross-country
skiing or snowboarding
hockey
tennis
swimming
volleyball
wrestling
gymnastics

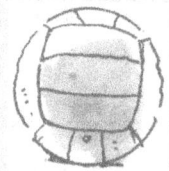

School Clubs and Groups
foreign language club
computer club
chess club
science club
math club
environmental club
book group
school yearbook
school newspaper
band, orchestra, or chorus
drama
writers' group

Classes and Lessons for Kids
acting
dancing or singing
skating
guitar or another instrument
martial arts like karate
yoga
woodworking
babysitting
swimming
fishing
sailing, canoeing, or kayaking
juggling
cooking

Community Groups
Scouts
Boys and Girls Clubs of America
YMCA, YWCA, YHA
youth group at a place of worship

> 4H
> after-school programs
> summer programs

Choose Friends Carefully

Everyone wants good friends. They make us laugh. They do things with us. They let us know that we are okay. But often kids with behavior challenges have some friends who have too many **negative** behaviors. These friends do and say things that are mean or embarrassing. They hurt people's feelings and get in trouble. Sometimes they are good to be around, but other times they aren't. You probably already know if you have friends like these. Maybe they make things hard for you at times, or maybe you end up getting into trouble with them.

> ## 5 Things GOOD FRIENDS Do
>
> Here are some things good friends do. Kids who do these things are the kind of people **YOU** want to be friends with:

1. Good friends can be counted on. They call when they say they will. They keep secrets that their friends tell them. They listen and give good advice.

2. Good friends are loyal. They stand up for their friends when others say bad things about them. They make their friends feel welcomed, valued, and comfortable.

3. Good friends share. They share time and do things together. They share feelings, hopes, dreams, and opinions, too.

4. Good friends show respect. They play fair and take turns. They're good sports who make a game fun for everyone. They like their friends for who they are. They say nice things. Sometimes they might tease in a fun way, but not in a mean way. They know that a joke is only really a joke if both people laugh. If they disagree, they talk about it and work together to solve the problem.

5. Good friends help each other. They help their friends learn to do things. They cheer them on.

They talk with them. They also help their friends find trusted adults to talk to about problems.

When friendships are negative, it's time to find some new friends. This isn't always easy to do. You may be used to spending time with "problem" friends. They will probably want you to stay in their group and keep hanging out with them. Plus, to get good friends, you'll have to be on your best behavior. You'll have to make smart choices. It's worth it!

IT'S YOUR TURN

- **Think of someone who's a GOOD FRIEND. What makes him or her a good friend?**
- **Which qualities do you have right now that make YOU a good friend?**

- What could you work on so you could become a better friend?
- Do you have any "problem" friends? What can you do to find better friendships?

REMEMBER...

Maybe you have lots of good friends already.

Maybe you don't yet, but you are trying to make some new ones. Even if this is hard at first, you can do it! Use the ideas in this chapter. Also use the skills you've learned for getting along with adults. Talk and listen. Show respect. Be assertive. These things can all help you in your friendships.

You are learning lots of ways to change your behavior. You are working on making good choices. One really good choice is to decide to make good friends and to be a good friend. The skills for making and keeping friends will also help you be a success in life.

160

CHAPTER 8

Ways to Help the Adults at Home Help YOU

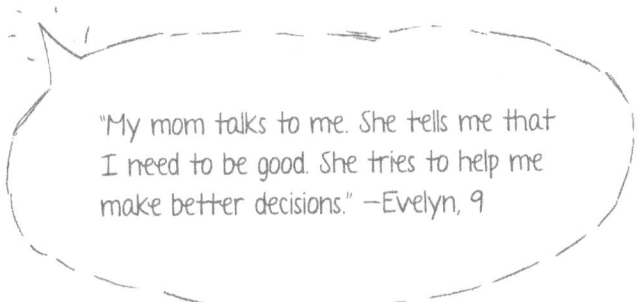

"My mom talks to me. She tells me that I need to be good. She tries to help me make better decisions." —Evelyn, 9

> **Remember, when you read about *family adults, parents,* or *adults at home,* think of the adult or adults who live with you and take care of you. This might be one or two parents, stepparents, foster parents, guardians, relatives, or others. It's different for each kid.**

Ahhh. It's great to be home ... or is it? Sometimes the grown-ups at home (and the kids, too) don't understand the challenges of having behavior challenges. When kids make good and bad choices, family adults might not react like teachers do. They don't know how hard it can be to make the right decisions. Some parents think their kids with behavior challenges should make smart choices every time. Sometimes they don't know how hard their kids are working to do this. Sometimes they forget to pay attention to the good choices their kids make. And they get mad when kids still make some bad ones. Some of these adults think that the kids are just being lazy. Maybe they even think kids are making bad choices on purpose.

Some parents are very good at helping their kids make better choices. Others haven't learned the best ways to do this. Read what these kids say about how adults at home try to help them behave better:

"They punish me. I can't watch TV or play video games. They won't let me go places."

"My stepmom does homework with me to make sure I get it done."

"With my new foster parents, I get to go see my grandfather if I have a good week."

"My dad tells me I need to be good."

"My mom's boyfriend tells my mom to 'get tough' with me. He's always yelling at me and bossing me around. When I do what he says, he tells me that I did it wrong. That makes me mad. Sometimes I ignore him and walk away. Sometimes I get so upset that I yell back at him. That really gets me in trouble."

"I live with my grandma. She loves me a lot and does nice things for me. But when I make mistakes, she gets really mad and says I'm no good. It really hurts me when she says these things. I get afraid she won't let me stay with her anymore. Then I try to do nice things for her. But she stays mad for a long time."

You're trying to make good choices. It feels awful when the grownups you live with don't understand this. It's easier to change when others help you. But sometimes kids who have behavior challenges don't get much help at home. They have to work on making better choices all by themselves. You **CAN** make changes yourself. That is something to be very proud about. As you do, you can start to help family adults help **YOU.** This chapter will give you ways to do that. It has ways to help no matter how well or not-so-well the adults handle things right now. The ideas can also help you get along better with others at home, like sisters and brothers.

Use Talking and Listening Skills

Many kids with behavior challenges have problems talking about things with the grown-ups at home. Remember the skills you've been practicing, like I-talk (Chapter 4) and request sandwiches (Chapter 6). People listen when others talk to them in a nice way. This shows respect. Help people at home (the adults *and* the kids in your family) understand what you're doing or how you're feeling. Do this by talking to them in a polite and friendly way. When they answer you, listen to what they say. Then you'll understand what they're thinking, too.

Always look for solutions. Remind yourself that yelling and arguing don't help solve problems. They usually make problems worse. When people argue, they get mad. They may get so mad that they say really mean things. Also, with an angry argument, no one can listen very well. Then no one really hears what the other person is saying. The same arguments happen over and over. The grown-up doesn't think about what you are trying to say. You don't think about how the adult feels. People need to work *together* to make things change. **Fighting can' t help** make things better. **Talking can.**

Use I-talk. It's hard to keep calm and talk nicely when people don't agree with you. It takes some practice, too. But it's worth it! Try to talk about what happened and how everyone feels about it. Don't blame others. That keeps them from listening to you. Instead, use I-talk to explain how you feel and what you want. (If the others use you-talk, do your best not to notice. They may not know about I-talk like you do.) Together, talk about how to solve the problem (so it doesn't happen again, or happens less). Work on solutions. Usually both sides need to change some things. Then do your part to make things better.

What if talking doesn't seem to work? You could ask (nicely), "What would you like me to do to solve the problem?" Listen to what your parent (or brother or sister) would like you to do. Decide if you could do it. If it sounds like a good choice, do it. If it doesn't, see if you can think of another idea that would be okay with everyone. Ask if you could do that instead. Later, be sure to let the other person know that you did what you said you would do.

These things are easy to say, but not so easy to do. Adults may want perfect behavior. **Hey, nobody's perfect!** But you are working hard on making better choices. Explain how you are working to do this. You might even have to tell about a time when you *did* make a better choice. That might help family grown-ups notice your smart choices more. Tell them you'll keep working to improve. Say you'll do this because you want to get along better and stay out of trouble. You can also tell them you want them to feel good and proud about **you.** Tell **them** you are working hard to make all these good things happen.

IMPORTANT!

Talking nicely can help you avoid arguments. But what if adults at home yell and fight with you no matter what you do? What if a grown-up's anger is out of control? If the fighting is really bad or you are scared or unhappy at home, talk to another grown-up. See the list of adults to talk to see "Adults You Might Talk To". Ask one of these people for help.

If trying to talk nicely doesn't work, show this book to the grown-ups at home. Point out the ideas you have read about for working together better. Tell them how the book is helping you meet your challenges.

Ask for Help with Your Goal

Tell the adults at home what behavior goals you are working on. Ask them to watch for those behaviors. Ask them to notice and say something nice when you do the right things. Ask them to remind you when you should be making a better choice. When they remind you, say thank you. Be sure to do that better thing **right away.** Then they will know that you really are trying to make a change.

Ask What the Grown-Ups Want You to Do

Many adults tell kids what **NOT** to do. ("Don't do that!") It would be better for them to tell kids what they **DO want them to do.** If your parents tell you what to stop doing, be polite and ask them to say it in a different way. Ask them to tell you exactly what they would like you to do. They might answer, "Be good" or "Stay out of trouble." If they do, ask them to tell you the actions they want to see you show. Then you'll know exactly what behaviors they expect.

IDEA!

Find someone to play the part of an adult at home. Practice talking to the person about your goals and asking for help with them.

Ask for "Sandwiches"

Remember the request sandwich you read about in Chapter 6? Request sandwiches let you put your request between two nice things. Request sandwiches are a great way to ask adults to do something *you* want *them* to do. Here's another sandwich idea: a **compliment sandwich.**

Ask adults at home to use a compliment sandwich to talk to you about things *they* want *you* to do. Explain (nicely) how they can use three steps:

1. Ask or give you a reminder.
2. Tell you one thing they like about you. (This is the compliment.)
3. Remind you again.

The reminders are like the two pieces of bread in a sandwich. The compliment is like the cheese or tuna-fish salad that goes between them.

If grown-ups can use a sandwich like this, you'll know what to do right now. You will also hear a **good thing** about yourself.

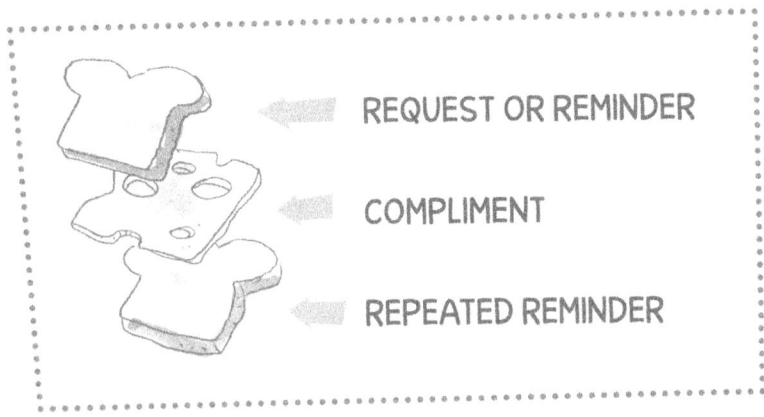

REQUEST OR REMINDER

COMPLIMENT

REPEATED REMINDER

Here is an example. Can you find the compliment between the two reminders?

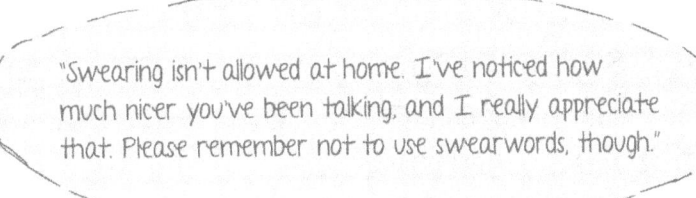

"Swearing isn't allowed at home. I've noticed how much nicer you've been talking, and I really appreciate that. Please remember not to use swearwords, though."

You can also ask for a **request sandwich.** (It's the one that starts and ends with nice things. The request or reminder comes in the middle.) That way you'll hear nice things about yourself twice! You'll do the right thing (or figure out how to make things better). Then your parent might use a request sandwich again next time. Here's an example:

SOMETHING NICE "You were really playing nicely with your brother at first. Thanks for being such a good brother."

REMINDER "But remember that he's a lot smaller than you. It really hurt him when he got tackled so hard."

SOMETHING NICE AGAIN "I know you'll be gentle with him from now on, just like you were doing before."

What will you do when you hear this? Apologize and play nicely with your brother again, of course!

So ask parents and other adults to use a "sandwich" when they want you to do something. If you want, show them the examples of request and compliment sandwiches in this book. Ask them in a friendly way. You could use your own request sandwich to do this:

> "It helps when you remind me to make good choices. Could you please tell me what I'm doing right, too? Like in this book? That would be great. Thanks for reminding me."

You can give sandwiches to other family members, too. You can give them to sisters, brothers, cousins, and visitors. After all, everybody likes to hear nice things about themselves. Plus, people are more likely to do what you want when you ask nicely. This almost always works a lot better than unfriendly words or a mean voice.

A Challenge for You

This is a challenge in two parts. Do it in your notebook, one part at a time. (When you're done, you can compare your ideas to the solutions in section entitled "Solutions to Some of the Challenges and Questions".)

CHALLENGE 1: Read the statements. Which one is a request sandwich? Which is a compliment sandwich? Which one is just a complaint?

1. "The dirty dishes are in the sink and it's your turn to do them. Be sure to do a super job on them just like you did last time. Do them now, please."

2. "You forgot to take out the garbage again. What's your problem? It's the only chore we ask you to do."

3. "I remember how great your room looked yesterday. But right now it looks like a tornado was in there. I know you'll make it look super again before dinner."

CHALLENGE 2: You are trying to put together a really hard jigsaw puzzle. Your sister wants to help you, but she puts pieces in the wrong places. She is breaking parts of the puzzle that you have put together, too. You feel upset. But you remember to use a sandwich and a nice voice to get her to stop. She is trying to help you, but you don't want the puzzle messed up. Make your own sandwich for this situation. It can be a compliment sandwich or a request sandwich.

Take a Time-Out

How can you avoid making bad choices when you get mad? Take a timeout. Stop yourself from doing anything wrong. Instead, say in a calm voice, "I need to be alone for a little bit." Then leave and go to a place where you can be by yourself. Go to your room. Go to the bathroom. Take a walk.

While you're alone, work on a solution. Instead of just being mad, try to think of a way to make things better. Think about what you will say or do the next time you see the adult (or kid) you have a problem with. **If you did some things wrong,** take responsibility for them. Apologize and promise to do better. **If it's not your fault,** can you think of a way to say what you need with I-talk? Can you think of a way to make a sandwich? Can you think of some things to suggest so the problem won't happen in the future? Think of how you will suggest things in a nice way so that everyone works together to solve the problem.

Ali

Ali lived with his mom. He knew she loved him. But his behavior challenges had made lots of problems for his mom. Ali was working hard on getting along better at home. He tried to show respect and talk nicely. He saw some small changes. His mom was nicer to him sometimes. Ali felt happy to see how his smart choices made his mom smile.

He wanted to get something special for her birthday. He told Mr. Hill, who owned the corner store. Mr. Hill said he would pay Ali to run errands. Ali helped Mr. Hill every day after school for two weeks. He made enough money to buy his mom some new cooking utensils. She was a great cook, but her utensils were bent and scratched. Even though she said they still worked just fine, Ali knew she would like new ones. So Ali went to a department store and bought some. He used the money he'd earned helping Mr. Hill. The clerk gave him a box for the new utensils. Ali decorated the box and made a card. He was excited about the gift.

On his mom's birthday, Ali handed her the gift. "Happy Birthday!" he said. She smiled and opened the box. Then her smile turned to a frown. "Where did you get the money to buy these?" she asked in an angry voice. "Did you take it from my drawer?"

Ali was very hurt and angry. He started to feel like screaming and hitting. But he knew that would make things worse. He tried to start telling his mom how he bought the gift. But she said, "Don't lie to me!" She wouldn't listen. So Ali took a deep breath. Tears came, but he said as calmly as he could, "I worked hard for those. Right now I'm gonna go to my room. Okay?" Mom said, "Yes. You get to your room now till I'm ready to deal with you!"

IT'S YOUR TURN

> - **Think about a time when you were arguing and no one was really listening to the other person. Pretend that it is happening again. This time, imagine taking a time-out to handle things better.**
> - **What words could you use before you leave the room for the time-out?**
> - **Where could you go to be by yourself?**
> - **What solution could you suggest when you talk to the person later?**
> - **What words could you use to suggest your plan? (Remember respect, I-talk, and sandwiches!)**

Ali sat on the bed and squeezed his pillow. He thought, "This is really unfair." He had wanted to surprise his mom. He had done the right thing and earned money for the present. But she thought he had stolen it. Even when she'd said this, Ali had made smart choices. He had stopped to think. He had used I-talk. He had taken a time-out. But Mom hadn't noticed any of that. In between his upset feelings, Ali tried to think about what to do next. How could he solve the problem?

He knew his mom would cool down after a while. She always did. He decided to wait until they both felt calmer. That night, his mom went out with a friend. In the morning, Ali went to school. He made good choices there. But he kept thinking about things at home. The next night, Ali's mom came home from work. She asked, "Ali, where did you get the money for my present?" He told her how he earned the money. He said she could ask Mr. Hill if she wanted to. He said all this in a respectful way. And he could tell that his mom believed him and felt bad. She said, "It's hard for me to learn to trust you, Ali. I'm happy about how you earned the money. And I like my gift a lot." Then she started to fix supper. Ali saw that she was using the new utensils.

Ali felt better. He started to think about more ways he could try to make things better at home.

Set Up a Point Sheet Together

Want a good way to remind adults at home to pay attention to the good things you do? And to remind yourself to do them? Try using a point sheet. You may already use a point sheet at school. There, point sheets have the goals for how you should behave in class. Here, you can have a point sheet with goals for good ways to act at home.

Score Points at Home

Scoring Key
0 Forgot goal or made bad choice
1 Did my goal behavior a little bit
2 Did my goal behavior pretty often
3 Met my goal!

My Goals for This Week

Goal 1: _Respect family_

Sun	Mon	Tues	Wed	Thurs	Fri	Sat
2	3	2	3	3	2	2

Goal 2: _Remove dishes from room_

Sun	Mon	Tues	Wed	Thurs	Fri	Sat
2	3	3	3	2	3	3

Goal 3: _Do chores without reminder_

Sun	Mon	Tues	Wed	Thurs	Fri	Sat
2	1	1	2	3	3	2

My Reward
Reward: _Trip to Burger Bob's_
Points needed for reward: _50_

You and your parent or guardian could set two or three goals for you to work on at home. Write them down on a form to use for a week. You can copy or print out the "Score Points at Home" form in below pages. Each week, you can use a new copy of the form. Every day, look at the goals together. Decide how many points, 0–3, you earned for each goal for the day. (3 means you remembered something every time and did a really good job.) Agree on what the reward will be. Also agree on a number of points that will earn this reward.

At the end of the week, add up your points. If you earned your reward, enjoy it! Make a new point sheet with some different goals for the next week.

If you didn't quite earn your reward, try again for another week. Keep trying to improve a little bit at a time.

Here's one other idea: You could look with a family grown-up at the "Five 'Tricks' to Help You Track Your Progress". They are ideas for school, but you could use some of the same ways at home. With the adult, figure out some ways to track your progress at home. Work together to make things better.

REMEMBER...

Sometimes the folks at home forget (or don't know) about how hard you are working to change your behavior. Be sure to tell family adults about smart choices you have made. Use the nice ways you have learned to remind them that you are trying to improve.

Keep using the ideas in this chapter. If you do, little by little things at home are likely to get better.

Don't expect things to change right away. And don't expect home to be perfect. (Remember, you're not perfect. And your family isn't, either.) No matter what, you can feel good that you're showing respect and making better decisions. Give yourself a BIG pat on the back for that!

And then ... keep reading. The next chapter has more ideas for making home a happier place to be.

Score Points at Home

Scoring Key

0 Forgot goal or made bad choice
1 Did my goal behavior a little bit
2 Did my goal behavior pretty often
3 Met my goal!

My Goals for This Week

Goal 1: _____

Sun	Mon	Tues	Wed	Thurs	Fri	Sat

Goal 2: _____

Sun	Mon	Tues	Wed	Thurs	Fri	Sat

Goal 3: _____

Sun	Mon	Tues	Wed	Thurs	Fri	Sat

My Reward

Reward: _____

Points needed for reward: _____

From *The Survival Guide for Kids with Behavior Challenges* by Tom McIntyre, Ph.D., copyright © 2013. Free Spirit Publishing Inc., Minneapolis, MN; 800-735-7323; www.freespirit.com. This page may be reproduced for individual, classroom, or small group work only.

For other uses, contact www.freespirit.com/company/permissions.cfm.

CHAPTER 9

More Ideas for Feeling Good at Home

> "I like being at home. I can relax and just be myself. I can do what I want. I don't have to worry about a teacher watching me all the time." —Lena, 12

When you're home, you want to be relaxed and comfortable. You want to take a break from the hard work in school. In other words, you want to feel "at home." It's hard to do this if you are having trouble getting along with people in your family. In Chapter 8, you read about ways to talk and listen to family adults. You found ideas for asking them to help you in positive ways. This chapter has some other "tricks" you can do to make things better at home. These are ideas that will help you:

- Show grown-ups at home the good choices you are making.
- Solve problems with the adults and kids in your family.
- Treat people the way you want them to treat you.
- Take care of yourself so you feel healthy and strong.

All of these ways can help **YOU** make home a happier place to be.

Tell Family Adults About Your Good Choices

Sometimes people forget to notice the good things that others do. They need to be reminded. That can be true with adults at home. Sometimes they only seem to notice bad choices, not smart ones. It's important to make fewer wrong choices. It's also important to help people at home notice the good things that you do.

Tell your parents when you do good things and make smart choices. If they don't show that they are happy, ask them what they think about your good choice. If you still don't hear what you want, give yourself credit just the same.

You did well and you know it. That's the **most important** thing.

> Remember, when you read in this chapter about *family adults, parents,* or *adults at home,* think about the grown-up or grown-ups YOU live with.

Be Sure Your Teachers Share Good News

Parents and guardians of kids who have behavior challenges often hear a lot more bad news than good news. Your parents have probably been asked to come to school to talk about when you made a poor choice. It is hard for them to hear this kind of news. They want you to do well. They need to hear more good things about you. Here are some ways to make sure this happens:

- Ask your teachers to tell your parent or guardian when you are doing better at making good choices. Ask them to make a phone call home or send notes with you when you've made lots of good decisions during the day.
- Ask grown-ups from home to ask your teachers for **good news.** They can explain to the teacher that they want to help with any problems that happen in school, but that they *also* want to hear about your **progress.** They can ask to talk about things that you have been doing better than before. That will remind teachers to say good things about you. Parents need to hear those good things. You

can also ask your parents to tell your teacher about **smart choices** you have made at home. Then your teacher will hear more good things about you, too.

Make a Plan to Solve Problems

What things seem to cause problems again and again at home? Is it doing your homework? Remembering to do your chores? Getting in arguments with your brothers or sisters? Think about what thing causes problems over and over again. Make a plan to handle the problem better. Then put the plan into action. Later, think about if your plan worked or not. If it worked, keep doing it. If it didn't work, think of a new plan and try it. The hard part will be remembering to use the new way in that situation. If you find yourself reacting in the same old way, stop. Then remember what you planned to do, and do it.

Renee

Renee has a problem doing her homework. She forgets to bring it home a lot. Other times, she brings it home but plays first, eats dinner, and then watches TV. By the time she thinks about doing the homework, she is feeling too tired. She knows that the teacher will be upset and give her a zero. She knows that her foster mom, Bev, will find out and be mad. Bev and Renee will probably have a big fight. Renee sees that getting her homework done can help her get along better at home.

What plan can Renee make to be sure that she gets her homework done each day? She needs to do two things:

1. **Remember to bring the homework home.** To do this, Renee might put a big reminder note where she'll see it. She could put it in her folder or pocket. She could tape it right inside her desk or locker. Maybe she could hook the note to her key ring. Renee could also ask her teacher or a friend to remind her each day. She could ask the teacher and classmates for ideas for ways to remember, too.

2. **Plan and take time to do it.** Having a set time to study every day can really help. Maybe Renee could do the work right after school. Maybe she'd rather play for an hour and then study. She might decide to do half the homework right after school, and half right after dinner. She could reward herself with a favorite TV show. The main thing she'll need to do is figure out a time and stick to it as much as she can.

When you think about it, Renee has lots of choices that could be good ones. Often there is more than one way to solve a problem. Sometimes, too, it takes more than one person to solve (and also to make) the problem.

Tom and Dino

Tom and his brother Dino argued a lot about which TV show or video game should be on the screen. They'd grab the remote control, yell, and fight. Their dad would come in and turn off the TV. Then neither of them got to watch or play.

Tom decided to see if he and Dino could try a plan to solve this problem. He took the TV schedule from the newspaper. The two boys looked at what was going to be on TV later. They joked and tried to make deals about which shows to watch that night. After a while, they agreed on some shows and times. (They didn't always get their first choice. They each had to give in a little.) They circled the choices. They even remembered to leave the TV free for their dad so that he could watch his favorite news program.

> ## IT'S YOUR TURN
>
> **Think of something that keeps causing arguments at home. Follow these steps:**
>
> **1. Think of all the ways that could help solve the problem. Write some of your ideas in your notebook. Be sure to think about some of the ideas and skills you practiced in Chapters 2–8.**
>
> **2. Choose an idea to try. Make a plan for solving that problem.**
>
> **3. Try it out and decide if it was a good plan or not.**
>
> **If your plan doesn't work, go back to your other ideas. Try another plan. Keep working on solving the problem.**

Coming up with a plan for computer games was harder. First they agreed that they would take 15-minute turns. But sometimes that was too short a time. The game was just getting going when it was time to stop. They had to find a better plan. They decided what to do if one of them couldn't stop at the 15-minute mark: The player could keep going for up to 10 minutes more. At that point, the person **MUST** stop the game. The other person would then get 10 minutes of extra time the next time he played. They made a chart to keep track of how many minutes they "owed" each other.

Do Kind Things for No Reason

Want to hear more good things about yourself? And feel better about **YOU?** One good way is to do nice things for others—even things you don't *have* to do. When you have some free time, think of something nice you can do for somebody in your family (or a neighbor). Anytime you're not really busy, look around for something nice to do for someone you like. It will feel great to do a good deed, even if the other person never finds out who did it. You can take pride in making someone happy.

Sometimes, your good deed won't make someone happy. Maybe the person you helped doesn't like part of what you did. What can you do then? Ask for a "sandwich." (Read about sandwiches.) Or ask (in a nice way): "Did you see that I was trying to help you?" Let's hope the person sees that you meant to be a big help. If not, say, "I'm sorry you didn't like what I did. I wanted to help." But don't give up on doing nice things for people. Most of the time, people are glad to be treated kindly.

Say "Thanks"

Another way to make things better at home is to notice the nice things other people in your family do. Isn't it great when someone cooks the meal? Wasn't it helpful of your big brother to get that game you wanted off of the top shelf for you and your friend to play? Wasn't it nice that your younger cousin drew a picture for you? Weren't you glad to be allowed another five minutes to play outside? Say **"Thanks."** Tell people who are nice to you what you like about what they did.

Here's another idea. Maybe you forgot to say thank you to someone who did something nice for you. When will you see the person again? Remind yourself to thank the person. You could even write it in a note.

Take Care of Yourself

What does taking care of **YOU** have to do with changing your behavior? Lots! When you are healthy and feel strong, many things become easier to do. It can be easier to think, make good choices, and solve problems. Really! Here are six important things you can do to take great care of yourself:

1. **Eat right.** Candy, snacks, soda, and other "junk food" can taste pretty good, but did you know that they make it harder to think? Healthy food actually helps your brain. It helps your emotions. It helps you think clearly. Make a promise to yourself to eat more of the healthy stuff. Ask if you can have vitamins, too. Take them every day. Start skipping junk food more often. (Or eat less of it when you do have it.) Your brain will thank you by helping you make better decisions.
2. **Take your medicines.** Sometimes kids with behavior challenges have medications to help even out the chemicals in their brain. When the chemicals are working right, kids find it easier to slow down or think

more clearly. If you have medicines to help you with your behavior challenges, be sure to take them. Follow the exact directions from the doctor. Taking your "meds" is important for making better choices.

3. **Keep your appointments.** Many kids with behavior challenges have regular appointments with people who work to help them. These people might be counselors, social workers, childcare workers, doctors, or others. They are adults who have had special training so they can help kids. It's important to show up for appointments. Let these people help you solve problems and make good decisions.

4. **Find a hobby to do at home.** A hobby is a great way to get your mind off of teachers and parents

for a while. You could start a collection. You might collect stamps, guitar picks, sports cards, bottle caps, pennies with different dates, rocks—anything that's interesting to you. Or think of something you would like to learn about or do. Choose something that makes you happy and is a good choice. Would you like to know more about how car engines work? If so, become an expert! Read about cars. Search online for information. Watch car races on TV. Build model cars. See if you can go to an auto show.

Maybe you could earn some money to spend (or save) for your hobby. You could collect soda cans and bottles to return to the store. You could put up signs telling others that you will cut grass, run errands, or clean windows. You could shovel snow in the winter, water plants in the summer, or walk neighbors' dogs. But before you decide on a job, be sure to talk it over with grown-ups at home. They will tell you if the job is a safe one for you.

5. **Find a place to relax.** Everyone needs some quiet time alone once in a while. Maybe you already have a spot at home where you go to daydream, read, or just be still. If not, think about where you can go. You could lie on your bed. You could rest in a corner or chair in the living room or bedroom. Maybe you'll sit in the closet for a while. Or find a tree outdoors to sit down beside. Find a spot where you feel comfortable and at ease. (It might be the time-out place you planned in Chapter 8.) When you need a quiet break, go to your place. Take a little time to breathe deeply and relax.

6. **Keep working on your self-esteem.** It's important to remember all the good things about yourself. Be proud of the things you do well and the smart choices you make. Notice the things you are doing better now than before.

Keep doing your pride and progress exercises and the "mirror talking" that you read about in Chapter 2. Doing these things will remind you of your good qualities and all the progress you are making.

REMEMBER...

You can't control everything that goes on at home (or school), but YOU can make a BIG difference. Your choices can make things better or worse. They can make it easier or harder to get along with other people. So work hard on making good choices and getting along at home. If you do, home will feel like a better place to be. Not only that, but it will be easier to make better choices at school. When you try your best at both home *and* school, you'll beat your behavior challenges even quicker. You've got power! Use it well.

CHAPTER 10

Six Winning Ways to Work Toward Positive Change

"My teachers and my family are proud of how I've changed my behavior. So am I." —Sabrina, 12

In this book, you've read many quotes about making changes (like the one above). All of the quotes are from kids who are working hard to beat their behavior challenges. All of the kids who said these things know that it is difficult to make good choices and improve behavior, especially if they have been making mistakes for a long time. Did you notice how many kids felt good about the choices they have made?

Changing your behavior can be hard, but it's worth it. After all, it feels great to know you can keep making progress. It also feels great to look forward to middle school or high school knowing that you're ready to join activities, make friends, and learn new things. And most of all, it feels great to take charge and make your own life better.

Some kids who have behavior challenges don't want to try so hard to beat these challenges. They like to think that their problems will be over when they grow up and leave school. They think that when adults aren't telling them what to do, everything will be okay. But that's not true. In fact, these kids are very wrong.

Adults have lots of responsibilities. For example, they have to hold a job. They have to show up at work almost every day. (More days than school!) They always have to be on time. They have to follow their boss's directions and do their jobs well. And they have to get along with the other workers. Gee, it sounds a lot like school, doesn't it? Yep, school prepares you for your future in many ways.

That's why it's so important to learn to make smart choices now, not later. What happens when kids who have behavior challenges leave school without learning to make better choices? They face lots of problems. They are more likely to get in big trouble. They might even end up in jail. They usually make less money than other people. They have problems getting along with girlfriends, boyfriends, husbands, wives, kids, bosses, people they work with, and friends. These are facts from research studies that have been done.

Your future starts now! How well you do in the future depends on the choices you make today. In the other chapters in this book, you learned ways to make smarter choices. This chapter is about getting a positive attitude. It gives ideas to help you get and keep a mind-set that will make you a success.

1. Remember the Golden Rule

There's an old saying that is heard all over the world:

"Do unto others as you would have them do unto you."

This is known as the **golden rule.** You might hear people say it in different ways, but it always has the same meaning. It means that we should treat others the way that we would like to be treated. You can't expect to get respect unless you *give* it, too.

Here's another old saying: "What goes around comes around." Can you figure out what that means? Think of it this way: What you send out to others is what usually comes back to you. If you shout at others, do they usually smile and say something nice in return? Well, they might (if they remember the golden rule). But more often they probably shout back. If you treat others badly, will you get the respect you want? Probably not. To use another old saying: "You can't pick corn if you planted taters."

Prove your **inner strength** by refusing to treat others in a bad way. Show respect to other people even if *they* forget *their* manners. You can still stick up for yourself in that firm-but-kind (assertive) way you learned about in Chapter 4. Remind yourself to act the way you want others to act toward you. Keep your behavior "golden." That will help you build a future as bright and shiny as gold!

2. Take Responsibility for Your Actions

Everyone makes bad choices now and then. Your challenge is to keep working on making fewer.

Before you act, ask yourself: "Will my action make things better?" **Better** means that everyone feels respected and listened to. Your friends stay your friends. You keep out of trouble, look mature, and can be proud of your behavior.

> ## IT'S YOUR TURN
> - **Think of a time when you did something wrong, but said you didn't do it (or blamed someone else). Pretend that you are back in that situation. Act it out with a teacher or a friend. This time, take responsibility. What will you say? You can give a short excuse, but be sure that you say that you were wrong and won't do it again.**
> - **After that, think of what you would do in that situation if it happened again today.**

When you DO choose a wrong behavior, it's important to "own up" to it. This means you admit to making a bad choice. It means you know that you have control over your behavior. And it means that you're able and willing to change it. "Owning up" shows that you are taking responsibility for what you do! You're becoming powerful and in control of yourself.

Sometimes people say, "He made me do it" or "She made me angry." Those are excuses (poor ones).

Someone who blames others gives his or her power and control away to others. Making excuses tells your teachers that they need to help you get that control. So take responsibility for the choices you make. You'll still make some mistakes, even when you are good at making choices. We all make mistakes. What then? Admit it. Try to make things better. Avoid the mistake in the future. Take charge of your behavior.

Others respect you if, when you mess up, you make an apology. Say, "I goofed. I'm sorry." Say you didn't really mean it, or that you wish you'd done something else. Later, think of why the way you behaved was wrong and what you should have done instead. Then practice the right way to do it so that you'll remember to use that way next time.

What if you make a mistake, really didn't mean to do it, apologize, and still get yelled at? You could have this reply ready: "I admitted that I was wrong and said it won't happen again. I mean that." (Did you notice the I-talk?) Of course, now you'll really have to be sure that you don't do it again. (Or stop yourself quickly if you start to make that bad choice again.) Then people will see that you are truly working on changing your behavior.

On below pages is a form you can copy or print out called "Taking Responsibility for Choices." Use the form to help you figure out how to own up to a wrong choice you have made, fix things if possible, and do better in the future.

IDEA!

Apologize to someone you have caused a problem with. Practice your apology ahead of time. Before you go, think of something friendly you could do to make things better. Maybe you can give the person something you made, or do something nice for her or him.

3. Be Patient and Persistent

You are used to doing things in certain ways. Change will take time. Be patient with yourself. And be

persistent—keep trying. It will also take time for others to believe that you are really serious about changing your ways. You'll have to keep making good choices for a long time before people say, "Gee, this kid has changed." Then *they'll* change the way they act toward you. In the meantime, be patient with these people, too. You will keep working on better behavior. They will start to notice.

A Challenge for You

Here are a couple questions to think about:

1. What makes a smart choice different from a bad choice?

2. How are the results of smart choices different from the results of bad ones?

In your notebook, list some of the things that tell you when you've made a good (smart) choice. (When you're done, you can compare what you wrote with some of the possible answers listed in section entitled "Solutions to Some of the Challenges and Questions".)

4. Learn from Experience

Everything that happens to you can teach you something. Every mistake has a lesson in it, a lesson about life and choices. Take a moment when you are feeling calm after upsetting situations. Ask yourself what you can learn from these experiences. Think about what better choices you will make next time. Your **self-talk** can go something like this:

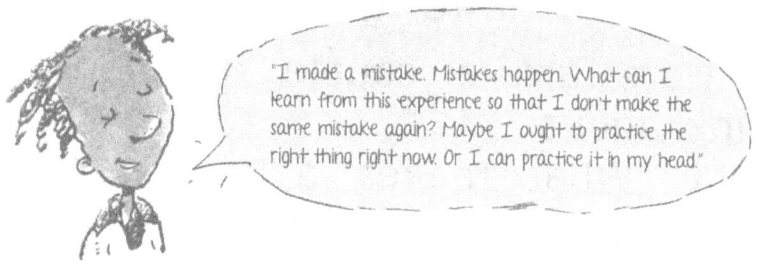

"I made a mistake. Mistakes happen. What can I learn from this experience so that I don't make the same mistake again? Maybe I ought to practice the right thing right now. Or I can practice it in my head."

5. Think About Your Future

You know that right now you are preparing for your future. School prepares you for being an adult. Activities outside of school prepare you, too. In school, you get an education about things like math, reading, and writing. (These are things you need to know to be good at just about any job.)

You learn how things work. You learn to follow directions so that work is done well and everyone stays safe. You learn to team up with other people, solve problems together, and get things done. Right now, you may even be learning about something that could lead to a future job that you will like to do. That's great!

IT'S YOUR TURN

In your notebook, start a list of jobs that sound interesting to you. Then choose a job. It can be anything, from a police officer to piano teacher, or a train conductor to a shoe repair person. Or choose a job area (for example, crime prevention or music). Do some research about the job or job area. Use books and magazines, the Internet, or videos about careers. Also talk to real workers who have those jobs. Learn things like this:

- **What do the workers do every day on the job?**

> - **What skills do they need so that they can do their job well?**
> - **What did they need to learn in school to do that job well? Read? Write? Do math? Be polite? Work well with others?**

Maybe you're nine, or eleven, or thirteen years old. These are all good ages for thinking about your adult career. Have you thought about what jobs you might want to do someday? Veterinarian? Restaurant owner? Lifeguard? Counselor? Bus driver? Teacher? Music store manager? Lawyer? Computer technician or programmer? Social worker?

Don't know? Think about the kinds of things you like to do. For example:
- Maybe you enjoy drawing. Cartoonists, book illustrators, architects who plan buildings, graphic artists who design things like logos and charts, and clothing designers are all people who draw in their work.
- Maybe you enjoy a sport. It's not just those star players who have

careers in sports. So do coaches, team managers, game officials, physical therapists, sport psychologists, and reporters.
- Maybe you really like animals. Some animal lovers work at pet stores, zoos, or animal shelters. Others become marine biologists, dog or horse trainers, or professional pet-sitters.
- Maybe you like to read and write. This book needed lots of people with those skills. There was the author, readers, editors, reviewers of books for magazines and websites, and librarians who decided whether to put this book in their library.

Start to notice and learn about jobs. Ask different people you meet about their work. See if you could spend a few hours with someone at his or her job. Or volunteer at workplaces that interest you. (Ask a teacher or family adult to help you figure out how to do this.) Find out how different workers chose their jobs. See which people like (and don't like) their jobs, and ask why.

Maybe you know exactly what you want to do as an adult. Maybe you have no idea yet. (If this last is true for you, don't worry. You will figure this out in time.) Either way, working to change your behavior is important for that future. The main reason people get fired from jobs isn't because they can't do the work. Most people can be trained to do the job. Most people get fired because they behave in an unsafe way, fail to follow directions, or don't get along well with others. So, the work you're doing now to make smart choices is getting you ready for any job you'll do later in life.

6. Know That You CAN Meet and Beat Your Challenge

The road to a positive future can be a long and difficult one. It's filled with bumps, detours, and roadblocks that may distract you from your goal. You have to work hard to stay on the path. You have to keep trying and never give up. **YOU CAN DO THIS!** If you believe in yourself and how you *can* change, you will complete your journey. You will look back with pride at what you have accomplished. That reward—and others—will make the trip worthwhile. If you stumble, pick yourself up, dust yourself off, and move forward again. Each step brings you closer to a brighter future.

Read what some kids with behavior challenges said about the progress they have made:

"I'm calming down quicker when I get angry. I get back to activities sooner."

"I've learned to control my temper better. I'm in charge of what I do now. With a cool head, I can listen to others and be listened to."

"I'm working on showing more self-control. I'm doing better at following directions and listening when the teacher is teaching."

"I've learned to read and to behave better."

"I'm proud of my behavior grades that keep getting better because I'm meeting my goals."

IDEA!

Make an "I Can" sign. Use a big piece of cardboard to make a large sign. Make a title like "I can do it!" at the top. T hen write these things:

I CAN DO IT

I will always do my best and will keep trying until I succeed.

If I make a mistake, I will take responsibility for what

I have done and try to make things better.

I will treat others as I would like to be treated.

I will appreciate kindness from others and say "Thank you."

I will believe in ME!

Place the sign somewhere at home where you will see it and think about it. Also write the words inside your notebook.

WHAT'S NEXT?

If you're in a regular classroom and not getting special help from counselors, psychologists, social workers, or special education teachers, you have reached the end of the parts of this book written for you. You are welcome to keep reading if you wish to do so. I hope that you will, because there are more good ideas there.

The next three chapters are written for kids who need a lot of special help to change their behavior and make better choices. To get these kids the help they need, schools have given them a label like "behavior disordered" or "emotionally disturbed." Now the schools can give them the special assistance they need to change their behavior for the better. If you are getting special education help, the next few chapters will answer a lot of the questions that kids in your situation often ask.

If you don' t have the label BD, you can still read these chapters. They can help you think about some of the reasons you could be making wrong choices. They can give you more ideas for being successful in meeting your challenge.

If you decide not to read Chapters 11, 12, and 13, that's okay too (as long as you think that's a good choice). You can go ahead and jump to section entitled "And Now..." where I have a final message for you.

Taking Responsibility for Choices

Use this form when you have made a wrong choice at school, at home, or somewhere else.

FIRST, ask yourself these questions:

1. What wrong choice did I make?

[Space left intentionally blank in original book]

2. What happens when this rule is broken?

[Space left intentionally blank in original book]

3. Would I like to be treated the way I treated the person or people involved?

Explain:

[Space left intentionally blank in original book]

4. What was I trying to do or get when I chose the wrong behavior?

Did my choice get me what I wanted?

[Space left intentionally blank in original book]

5. How could I get what I wanted in a way that wouldn't hurt anyone or get me in trouble?

[Space left intentionally blank in original book]

SECOND, decide what to do now to make things better. Check one or two choices. Then DO them!

_ Apologize to _____

_ Write a note to _____
_ Do something nice for _____
_ Make an appointment to talk with _____
_ Do nothing right now, but remember to make the right choice from now on. Practice the right choice right now.
_ Something else: _____
[Space left intentionally blank in original book]

From *The Survival Guide for Kids with Behavior Challenges* by Tom McIntyre, Ph.D., copyright © 2013. Free Spirit Publishing Inc., Minneapolis, MN; 800-735-7323; www.freespirit.com. This page may be reproduced for individual, classroom, or small group work only. For other uses, contact www.freespirit.com/company/permissions.cfm.

SPECIAL SECTION

What If You Have Been Given a BD Label?

> "I used to have a nasty attitude about everything. I finally listened to what my grandpa always said to me: 'If you're gonna have an attitude, at least make it a good one.' Things are better for everyone now that I'm in charge of my behavior." —Anton, 11

If you're reading this part of the book, you probably have a **BIG** behavior challenge in front of you. Your school has tried different ways to help you make better choices. Those ways worked for other kids, but they didn't always work so well for you.

Now the school is moving to the next step in helping you with your challenges. After a great deal of investigation and lots of meetings, people at the school have decided to give you a label. By law, they had to give you (or your behavior) this label so that they could also give you extra help. Professionals who work with kids who have BD don't all agree on which label to use—even when they're talking about the same kid! Doctors use different names than teachers. Teachers use different labels than **psychologists.** Even different schools will use different labels. But some common labels are **behavior disorder (BD), emotional or behavioral disorder (EBD),** and **emotional disturbance (ED).** (You'll find the official meanings for these terms in the glossary.) In this section of the book, I'm going to use the label "BD."

The people in your school care enough about you and your future to spend extra time and money helping you succeed. They have brought in people with special training to help you make positive changes. They are giving you "supports" or "special education services" that aren't available to most kids. The things that special education professionals do for you have helped other kids with BD learn to make smart choices.

It can be embarrassing to be given the BD label. But there is a good side, too: It lets you know that it is time to make changes in your life, while you have all these helpful people working with you.

In the next few chapters, you'll find out more about what the BD label means, the causes of BD, and how people in your school will work with you to make positive changes and solve your behavior issues.

CHAPTER 11

What Is BD?

"BD is a label. I don't like it. But at school, I'm learning ways to behave better." —Julio, 11

What Does BD Mean?

That's a good question. Earlier in the book, I said that **BD** stands for **behavior disorder.** But what does it **really mean?** If you have been labeled or diagnosed with BD (or one of the other labels that mean the same thing), it means that your behavior is getting in the way of learning at school for you *and* for other kids. It's making it hard for you to get along well with others. Your parents might also think it's causing trouble in your family. The school is using special ways to help you learn to make better choices. The behaviors that teachers and other school adults are trying to teach you will also help you in other ways. They'll help you get along better with your family and other kids. These new ways of acting will help you later, too. They'll help when you go to middle school or high school. They'll help you get a good job (and keep it). They'll even help you be a good parent when you are an adult.

The challenge for all kids with BD is to learn to make better choices. Choices about which behaviors to show at school, at home, and in other places. Choices about which words and actions will help them get along with teachers, parents, and other kids. Choices that will help them enjoy life more.

It's important to know that being labeled BD is not a punishment. You were given the label BD because teachers want you to be a success in life. They want to be sure you get special help so you can make better decisions about what to do in different situations.

IDEA!

Think about a behavior challenge you have—a situation where you often make the wrong choice about what to say or do.

What is **ONE** better thing you can do the next time you are in that situation?

Talk about this with your parent or a friend you trust. Or think about it on your own. Promise yourself that you will do that one better thing next time. Write your promise in your notebook or journal. T hen make sure that you work to keep that promise.

It's also important to remember that being labeled BD can mean different

challenges for different kids. Not everyone has BD in the same way.
- Some kids with BD have trouble obeying rules or following directions.
- Other kids find it hard to sit still or pay attention.
- Some have trouble making friends.
- Some have hurt others with their words or their bodies.
- Others are very shy.
- Others feel sad almost all the time. (This is called **depression.**)
- Some kids have to work on telling the truth.
- Some kids have one of these challenges, or two or three of them. Some may have all of the challenges. It just depends.

What BD Does NOT Mean

It can be hard to explain exactly what BD means. But there are some things that it definitely does *not* mean.

BD does NOT mean you are "bad." Yes, sometimes people may call you "bad." They are very upset at a behavior they have seen. They wish you had made a better choice. But it is not right to call you a bad person.

A better thing for them to say would be, "You are a good kid, but the behavior is bad and it needs to stop." Or, "I like you, but I don't like that behavior." The reason you're making wrong choices is because you *learned* wrong choices or because you are *feeling* bad—it is **NOT** because *you* are bad. But you can learn to make better choices and handle your feelings better. As you do this, people won't get so upset and they'll stop saying these hurtful and terrible things to you. Your smart behavior choices might even help other people see their own bad behaviors and wrong choices!

BD does NOT mean you are "crazy." People who are "crazy" have no control over what they do. You have control now over many behaviors. And you will learn to have control over other ones soon. When people see someone make wrong choices about behavior, they sometimes use words that hurt—words like "crazy," "weird," and "nuts." As you learn to make better choices about your behavior, you won't hear those angry, hurtful words so often. It will take time before people know that you have really changed your ways. So you'll have to make the right choices for quite a while before people notice.

IT'S YOUR TURN

• **What hurtful things have people said to you? Why do you think they said those things?**

• **Have you figured out a helpful thing to say or do when someone says mean things to you? If so, what do you do?**

BD does NOT mean you are "retarded." In most schools, having BD means that you take part in **special education (special ed).** Some kids might unkindly call students in special classes "retarded." Those kids—and even some grown-ups—may also assume that all students in special ed learn very slowly. That is not true. Kids get special ed help for many different reasons. You get special help because of your behavior, not because your brain is slow. If it *feels* like you're learning too slowly, this is probably because you need to make better choices about listening, following directions, and working on assignments. You might have a **learning difference (LD)** as well. This is true for some kids with BD, but not all. (You can read more about that in Chapter 12.)

It's Tough to Be a Kid with BD

That's the truth! Years ago, I did a study with two other teachers. We asked a group of kids who were labeled BD a few questions. One question was:

"How do other kids react when they find out you're in special education?"

Here are some of the answers we got:

"Some of them laugh and I get angry."

"They tease me."

"Some kids understand and some don't."

"They think I'm slow or stupid, but I'm not. That's why I'm quiet about it."

"They think that I'm bad or crazy."

"They start calling me names."

Another question we asked was:
"How do you feel about being labeled BD?"

These were some kids' replies:

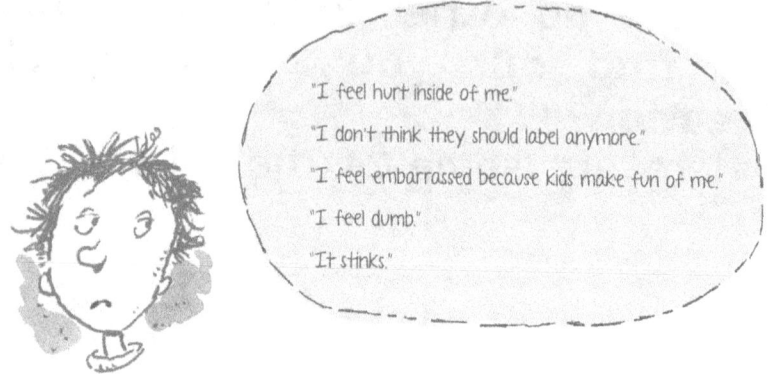

"I feel hurt inside of me."
"I don't think they should label anymore."
"I feel embarrassed because kids make fun of me."
"I feel dumb."
"It stinks."

Like most kids with BD, you probably wish you didn't have it. Teachers and other adults tend to get upset about it. Other kids might make fun of you or might not want to be friends with you. Plus, changing the way you behave in different situations is really hard. It can seem easier to just keep acting in the same old ways, but then you won't get the rewards you're working toward.

Even when you try the different ways, those ways sometimes don't feel right because they are new to you. (Remember that activity in which you folded your arms in two different ways? Remember how odd one of the ways felt? But with practice, it gets easier to do and feels more comfortable.)

> **IT'S YOUR TURN**
>
> • Have you ever made the right choice, but no one noticed—or people still treated you badly? Tell what happened in that situation.
> • What did you do then?
> • What is a helpful thing you can say or do the next time something like this happens?

People don't always give you the reaction you want from them, either. They might not notice how you're trying to change. Or maybe they notice, but they don't let you know this. Your challenge is to keep believing that if you make better choices, things will get better for you as time goes on.

Don't Use BD as an Excuse

Some kids with BD use their label as an excuse for making poor choices. They say things like:

Yes, changing your usual ways to other ways that will someday be your usual way is difficult. But it will happen faster if you take responsibility for your choices (good ones and bad ones). You can get better at making smart choices. Change excuses like "I can't help it" to words like:

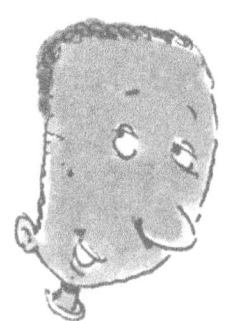

REMEMBER...

It's no fun to be labeled. But if you are, you get special help at school from people who are

trained to work with kids who have BD. And you can do your part to work on changing how you act at certain times. As you keep working, things will slowly improve for you. Getting along well at school, with other kids, and at home will become easier. You will find that you like yourself a lot more. That may be the best thing of all!

CHAPTER 12

Different Kids, Different Causes for BD

"I used to lose my temper a lot and wanted to scream. My mom just yelled back. But now my foster parents and teachers are helping me take responsibility. I don't want to let BD mess up my life." —Anne, 13

Do all kids with BD have the same behavior challenges? Nope! There are many types of BD. There are many reasons why kids have BD. And there are many ways that adults help kids make better choices.

It's difficult to be sure about the exact cause of a kid's BD. Still, it's usually possible to get a pretty good idea in most cases. This chapter talks about some common reasons why kids have BD. As you read, think about which reasons sound like they apply to you. You might find just one that fits your experience, or you might find more.

1. Kids Who Need to Learn How to Make Good Choices

Parents and other adults want kids to do well. But sometimes they don't know the best ways to help kids make the right choices about behavior. Other times, they try to teach kids the right ways to behave, but the kids don't catch on or don't learn them well. Sometimes, too, kids have learned to make wrong choices from adults who make wrong choices.

This means more problems when the kids come to school. Kids who haven't learned to make good choices have trouble getting along with others. They don't have the behaviors they need to follow school rules, learn well in class, or make new friends. Teachers try to help kids with BD make better choices.

The big challenge for these students is to work hard to learn new and better ways of acting.

Rodney

Rodney liked sports and enjoyed working on bicycles with his older brother. But he had problems making friends. He tried to talk and play with other kids, but he did things that they didn't like. He called them nasty names. He said things that he thought were funny, but that really weren't nice. He just didn't know how to meet people and make good impressions. Instead of liking Rodney, other kids stayed away from him. Rodney asked his teacher for help.

The teacher worked on helping Rodney become the type of person people like. Rodney and the other students in his special class took lessons in **social skills.** They learned about new ways to act. They practiced the ways together. Rodney worked very hard. He quickly learned ways to make friends and be liked by others. He made new friends slowly—not as fast as he would have liked to. Even though Rodney had better social skills, some of the other kids still didn't want to be friendly with him because they remembered some of the things he used to do.

Rodney didn't give up. He worked hard to follow rules and improve his grades. He kept getting better at making good choices. When he had been doing well for many months, he was allowed to take science and social studies in the regular classes. (He already took P.E. with kids in the regular education classes.) Then other kids got to be in groups with him, work on projects with him, and hear his answers in class. They saw that he behaved well and treated other people well. They thought that he was fun to be with and could be a good friend. It took persistence, patience, and hard work, but over time Rodney made lots of new friends. He got to be in even more regular classes. Pretty soon, all of his classes were regular ones. But his work wasn't over. He still checked in with the dean of students every morning and visited with his counselor twice a week. Learning to make better choices made a big difference in Rodney's life. He is a success story.

2. Kids Whose Brain Chemicals Are Mixed Up

Chemicals in the brain help people think and make decisions. Some kids have too much of one chemical or too little of another. This can make different things happen. It might make the kids move around a lot. It might make them feel really sad or get very mad at things that don't upset most other kids. It might make them see and hear things that are not really there. You probably know labels for some brain chemical mix-ups. For example, maybe you have (or know someone who has) a label like **ADHD** or **schizophrenia.**

Doctors sometimes give medicine to help with these kinds of conditions. The medicine helps the brain make the right amount of each chemical. This helps kids slow down, concentrate better, understand the world around them, learn more, and make better choices.

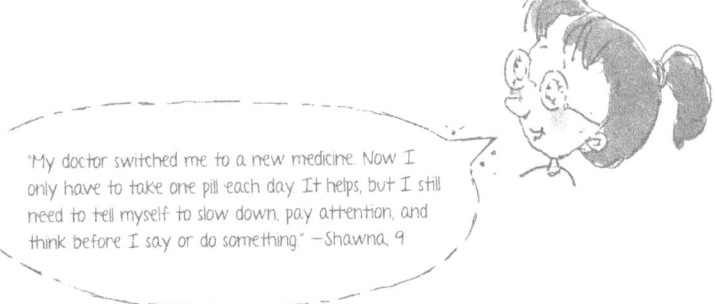

"My doctor switched me to a new medicine. Now I only have to take one pill each day. It helps, but I still need to tell myself to slow down, pay attention, and think before I say or do something." —Shawna, 9

One challenge for these students is to remember to take their medicine. These students may also have learned some wrong behavior habits. So even with the medicine, they often need to learn some new ways to act around teachers, friends, and family members, too.

3. Kids Who Learn in a Different Way

Some kids have trouble learning things the way that teachers usually teach in school. These kids may have a **learning difference or disability (LD).** Kids with LD often have trouble learning, but usually this is because they learn in a different way from many of the other students. For example, some kids with LD have trouble reading, but they learn really well if the teacher explains things and they listen instead of read. Or some kids may have trouble doing math, but they're great at reading. They can learn just fine when teaching is done in a different way.

When kids with LD struggle with something that's really hard for them, they may get mad at themselves. Or they might get mad at the work or at the teacher. They may start to act up. They might do things like rip up the paper or say, "I am not going to do this work." One ten-year-old student slammed books shut and told teachers "No!" when they asked him to read out loud. He would yell at the teacher, "I'm trying, but these books are too hard!" Teachers can get pretty upset about behavior like this. (Remember, it might seem like they're mad at the student, but it's really the behavior they don't like.) If the problems with learning go on, these kids might give up and not even try to do the work anymore.

The challenge for these students is to tell teachers that the work is hard and that they need special ways to learn better. Students with LD can work with their special ed teachers to figure out how they learn best. Then they can explain this to their regular teachers and to other adults who help them with learning. These students may also have to study more than other kids. This can be frustrating! The ideas in this book can help kids with LD make good behavior choices. Then wrong words and actions won't get in the way of the progress they are making with their learning.

4. Kids Who Want Attention

Sometimes parents and teachers don't tell kids when they are doing things right. These adults think that kids should "just behave." They forget that we all like to be noticed when we are doing the right thing. If kids don't hear nice things very often when they work hard or do well, they may try to get attention in other ways. They might act up to get *some* kind of attention, even if it's not the good kind.

> "Calvin and I like to get on other kids' nerves when they're trying to work. It's fun to get them upset with us." —Ted, 10

Sometimes, students act up to get attention from other kids. They like the laughs they get or the things other kids say. Even if the other kids get annoyed instead of laughing, it feels good to be noticed. So these students keep using wrong behavior. They think it helps them fit in and feel important with classmates and friends. They're wrong. Irritating others will never make them friends. Interrupting the lesson will never make a teacher feel good about those behaviors.

The challenge for these students is to learn better ways to get noticed. It can seem nice to get attention for wrong behaviors, but usually kids who do this don't really feel very good about it inside. They know it feels better to get attention for **positive** reasons. They work hard to get the bigger, better rewards that come with smart behavior choices.

5. Kids Who Feel Angry and Want to Get Back at Someone

Some students want **revenge** when someone else makes them mad. They try to hurt the other person. They may tell rumors. They may yell awful things or hit the person. Or they may do some other behavior that really only makes things worse.

"If anyone laughs at me, I kick their butt." —Dante, 12

The challenge for these students is to learn how to control the feelings that lead to anger and choose better ways to deal with strong emotions. Schools can help these students with **counseling** and with lessons in **anger management.**

Some schools also help students stop being mad at each other with ways like **peer mediation** and **conflict resolution.** This book helps, too. It shows you helpful ways to deal with angry feelings. It gives you lots of ideas for getting along better with other people, too. (For help handling anger right now, turn to Chapter 3,.)

IDEA!

Ask your special ed teacher or guidance counselor to form a **support group** to talk about behavior problems and how to stop having them.

6. Kids Who Feel Bad About Themselves

Some kids don't like who they are. This can happen because of one of the reasons you read about already, or maybe for another reason. When kids don't feel good about themselves, they sometimes make poor choices. They might say or do bad things to themselves. They might avoid doing things or being with others. They might pick friends who make bad choices and then get in trouble with them.

The challenge for these students is to build their **self-esteem** so that they feel better about themselves. Building self-esteem can make it easier to choose right decisions instead of wrong ones. This book helps you improve your self-esteem and make more good choices. Teachers and counselors have ways to help kids improve their self-esteem, too.

> ## IT'S YOUR TURN
>
> **Think about the six different reasons why kids have behavior problems:**
> 1. **Some kids never learned to make good choices.**
> 2. **Sometimes the chemicals in the brain are mixed up.**
> 3. **Some kids learn in a different way than most people.**
> 4. **Some kids want attention.**
> 5. **Some kids feel angry and want to get back at someone.**
> 6. **Some kids feel bad about themselves.**
> - **Why do you think you sometimes make bad choices?**

> • **What challenges do you have to remember to work on?**

Maria

Maria didn't feel good about who she was. She was very shy and cried a lot. When her teachers would ask her what was wrong, she didn't really know what to tell them. Her mother gave permission for the school to have a psychologist talk with Maria and give her some tests. The psychologist thought that things would get better if Maria talked with a counselor a couple of times each week.

Sometimes Maria talked alone with Miss Brown, the counselor. Other times, a few other kids with the same kinds of problems were there. They would talk about the things that were happening at home and school that made them unhappy. They also worked on ways to feel better. Maria liked to meet with Miss Brown and the other kids. They understood her problems. They gave her words to explain to other people how she felt.

Over time, Maria smiled more in school. She spent more time with the other kids and could concentrate better on her schoolwork. The problems at home and school didn't go away like magic, but she was able to handle them better.

> ### REMEMBER...
> **All kids with BD are different, but there *are* a couple of things that they have in common. First, no matter what the cause is of the behavior problem that you're working to change, *it* happened to *you.* You did not ask for it. You did not do anything wrong to have it happen to you. Now, though, *you* are the one who has to do the work to get rid of your behavior challenges.**
>
> **You can be glad for the second way kids with BD are alike. All kids with BD—including you—have great potential. This means that it is possible for you to change things so that you have a positive future. With hard work and**

persistence, you can change the negative behaviors you show sometimes. By using the ideas in this book, and the suggestions of your teachers and counselor (if you have one), you can make changes. You can become a kid other students like. You can be a student who gets along well with teachers and doesn't get in trouble. Really. Yes—REALLY!

CHAPTER 13

Why Am I in a Program for Kids with BD?

"Mrs. Vang is my special class teacher. She knows how to teach me. I know what to do in her class. In the regular class, things are harder to figure out." —Adam, 10

Before 1975, many schools did not want to teach kids with BD. If students didn't follow the rules or if they made poor choices, the schools could kick them out. If parents wanted their children with BD to go to school, they would have to use their own money to pay a special school to teach them. In 1975, a new law was passed. Today, that law is named **IDEA.** Here are some important things the IDEA law says:

- All kids, no matter what kinds of challenges they have, must be allowed to go to school.
- All kids must be taught in the kind of classes that help them learn best. The school must try to figure out ways to make regular class the best place to learn. But sometimes, a student isn't ready for that place. Then that student learns in a **special classroom** with a special teacher. There the teacher works to help that student get ready for the regular classroom.
- Students with behavior problems must have their own special school program that will help them learn and behave better. That program is written in a long report called an **IEP.** Each student who is part of IDEA has his or her own IEP. There is even one part of the IEP that talks all about behavior. It's called the **BIP (behavior intervention plan).** The BIP gives the teacher ideas for helping you learn new ways to act and react.

- The school must use the best ways it knows to help kids with certain kinds of **special needs** learn better and make good choices.

In other words, schools must give you the help you need to make better decisions about behavior.

How Did the School Decide That I Have BD?

IDEA says that teachers should get help for kids who have behavior that:
- keeps them from learning **OR**
- keeps other kids from learning **OR**
- keeps the teacher from being able to teach

Remember, you may have a different label than BD. Section

> entitled "What If You Have Been Given a BD Label?" tells some of the other labels. If you have an IEP and are in a special class or program to help you with your behavior, the information here applies to you.

Before you got the label of BD, a teacher noticed that you were having problems making good choices about your behavior. The teacher and some other adults at school talked about ways to help you make good choices and show positive school behavior. The teacher tried these ways, but they didn't work very well. So another group of adults called the **IEP team** had to decide if you needed special education to learn better ways to act in school. People on the team collected lots of information from adults who know you. They also asked your parent or guardian if they could meet with you and give you some tests. Someone from the team may have come into your classroom to watch you for a while. This was so the person could see how well you followed directions, paid attention, got along with other kids, and did your work. Someone may have interviewed you.

Then the team invited your parent or guardian to a meeting to talk about how to help you learn and behave better. After this, the team wrote your long IEP plan. This plan goes in a folder in one of your school's offices.

What Is in My IEP?

All kids with special needs have an IEP plan in their school folders. Your plan tells your teachers how to teach you best and help you make choices that will bring success in school and life.

What Your IEP Says

The law says that the IEP must tell:
- what the tests and talks found out about your challenges and strengths
- how well you are learning and behaving in school right now

> - what type of services, supports, and assistance will help you learn best
> - goals for learning and behavior that teachers think you can meet in one year
> - ways to decide if you have met those goals

When the IEP team was gathering information, they also did something known as an **FBA (functional behavior assessment).** They tried to figure out the reason or reasons you were having trouble making smart behavior choices.

After the school figured this out, they wrote your **BIP (behavior intervention plan).** The BIP is another part of your IEP. It tells teachers the ways that should be used to help you make better decisions. The BIP must include positive ways to help you make better choices. These ways are called **PBIS (Positive Behavioral Intervention and Supports).** Your BIP can't just list a bunch of punishments for bad choices. (There may be some of these in your IEP, though.) The BIP has to include positive and respectful ways to change your behavior, and ways to reward you when you make good choices. There also need to be ways to treat you with respect if you make a bad decision. For example, one of the ideas in the BIP might be that you get a reward or prizes for meeting goals. Another might be that you work in a group with other kids. There you learn the skills you need to beat BD.

Once your first IEP has been written, the IEP team meets at least once each year to talk about how you have been doing at meeting your goals. When the team meets, they change the IEP, or make a new one, to keep helping you meet more goals. Sometimes kids come to the IEP meeting if their parents or guardians invite them.

You might not like your plan or the fact that you are in special education. But remember: People who care about kids and know how to help them have worked very hard to find the best ways to help you.

Rashid

Rashid had trouble sitting still. He also did things without thinking about them first. He didn't mean to break the rules or stop the lesson. But he just couldn't seem to help it. He also talked with other students when he was supposed to be working.

For the last two months, Rashid has been taking a pill before he comes to school. He takes another one later in the day. The medicine changes the chemicals in his brain, and helps him sit still and think before he acts. Rashid also carries a point card with him. His special class teacher gives him points if he behaves well. So do the art teacher, the gym teacher, the bus monitor, the playground supervisor, and the lunchroom attendant. When he earns enough points, Rashid gets a reward like extra time in the learning center or on the computer. Rashid's BIP described this point system.

IT'S YOUR TURN

- What goals does your IEP say you are supposed to be working on?
- What positive ways (PBIS) are your teachers using to help you?
- What would you like to have changed in your IEP?

The point card makes Rashid want to do well. He tries hard to follow the rules. And he's doing great. His teacher, Mr. Dradi, is thinking that maybe Rashid is ready to go to the regular classes for one or two subjects. Mr. Dradi will decide in a few weeks if he should tell the IEP team that Rashid is ready for this.

Why Aren't I in the Regular Education Class?

Some kids with BD spend all day in the regular education classroom. Other kids with BD spend all day in a special classroom or special ed school. Some kids with BD have a mix of special and regular classes.

When kids with BD are in the regular class for the whole day, they usually still get some help from a **consultant teacher** or **paraprofessional** who works in the room. Sometimes there are two teachers in a classroom. In that case, one of them has probably had college training in helping kids with special needs.

Or maybe these kids talk with a counselor a couple of times a week. The law says that kids with special needs have to be in the regular education classroom as much as they can handle well. This is called **inclusion.**

IDEA!

- Do you have questions about your IEP or about being in special education because of BD? T hen be sure to talk to your special education teacher, your counselor, or an adult at home.
- Do you think that there are better ways to teach you to make

good choices? Talk to some of these people about your ideas.

Kids with BD who aren't in a regular classroom all of the time are often in a **self-contained classroom.** This is a room where these students go to school for all (or most) of the day. Sometimes it is called a "special class," and all of the kids in the class have special needs of some kind. The teacher of this class has gone to college to learn how to help kids with special needs. Students in special classes might go to regular education classes for one or two subjects. Usually they start with art or gym. If they do well in those classes, they will get a chance to go into more regular classes.

If you are in a special class, your special ed teacher helps you learn ways of doing things that will help you succeed in school. These ways help you learn better and make smart decisions. They can also help you make friends more easily. If you learn these things well, you will be able to spend more time in the regular classroom. How much time? That depends on how well you are making choices.

Remember: You can't just promise to show good behavior in the regular class. You have to prove that you can do it first. To get into regular classes, you have to work hard and make good choices while you are in the special classroom. This is the **ONLY** way to get into the regular classroom. Once you do, you have to keep making good decisions if you want to stay there.

More About Rodney

You first read about Rodney in Chapter 12. Rodney was in a special class because he had BD. He worked hard to follow rules, improve his grades, and make good decisions about his behavior. After many months, Rodney was allowed to go to the regular classroom for gym, art, science, and social studies.

Rodney wanted to be in the regular classes all the time. He kept working hard in his special class and his regular classes. He made an effort to obey the regular teachers' rules and complete all the work. He was polite even when one of the teachers wasn't so nice to him. He kept getting along better and better with other kids. He earned respect from the teachers.

After another year, Rodney only had to go to the counselor twice a week. He also saw his school's dean of students for fifteen minutes each morning. He and the dean would check his homework. They would talk about his plan for the rest of the day. Then Rodney went to regular classes. He learned about all the good things that happen when people make smart choices.

Changes take time and persistence. It took Rodney a long time to go from a special class to regular classes. He had to work hard and be patient. At first, this might sound discouraging. Slow changes are often the best kind, though.

With slow change, you have a chance to learn and practice new behaviors step by step. You have time to get used to each new experience you have to deal with. It's easier to make small changes, one by one, than to try to do one big change all at once. You need to get comfortable with your new behavior. Your teacher needs to see that the changes you're making are real. Each thing you accomplish—like getting to go to a regular class for one subject, or figuring out how to get along with a certain teacher—brings progress. You'll keep getting small rewards on the way to the big one: being successful in beating your behavior challenges.

> ## IT'S YOUR TURN
> - **If you are in a special class, how do you feel about being in it?**
> - **Do you spend time in a regular class, too? If so, what do you like about it? What don't you like? Why?**
> - **What goals do you have in your class or classes? What are you doing to work on them?**

What If I Don't Want to Go Back to Regular Classes?

Some kids with BD don't want to go back to the regular classroom. They are happy in the special class. They learn well there. They get lots of attention, and they get along with others. They remember when they did not do well in the regular class. Some are afraid that other kids will tease them. They worry that the work will be too hard. They don't know if they will get the help they need in the regular class. The IEP team's job is to figure out how to make the regular classroom a place where you can be happy and successful.

Tyrone

Tyrone never liked being labeled BD. He wanted to be in a regular class. When he started his special all-day class, he hated it. But after a couple of months, he was starting to like it in a lot of ways. He liked the way the teacher (Mrs. Mercado) and the assistant teacher (Mr. White) treated him. He was learning quicker, too. He still wanted to get back to the regular classroom, though. So he worked hard to change his behavior. He worked at this for almost two years. His behavior improved slowly all the time.

Then, partway through sixth grade, Mrs. Mercado said she had good news. She told Tyrone that the IEP team was talking about moving him back into the regular classroom. When Tyrone heard this, he had mixed feelings. Yes, he wanted to go back to regular classes. That was the dream that he had worked so hard for. But he liked being in Mrs. Mercado's class. Without help from Mrs. Mercado and Mr. White, could he keep making good choices? Could he do the work? Would kids in the regular class be friends with him? Would they make fun of him?

Tyrone hadn't even moved to a regular class, but he was very worried about it. Then he started to mess up. He began picking on weaker kids. He showed up late for class. He stopped doing his assignments. He began getting in trouble in the hallways, too. His teachers were confused. So was Tyrone.

Mr. White and Mrs. Mercado talked with Tyrone about why he was making so many bad choices all of a sudden. They asked if he really wanted to go into regular ed. He said he didn't know anymore. He told them that he was scared in some ways.

Talking about things helped Tyrone handle the stress and make sense of what was going on. He saw that he was comfortable in the special class. He didn't know how things would go outside of it. The teachers explained that he would only be in two classes to start. If things were going okay, then he could be in more regular classes later. Mrs. Mercado would talk with the teachers about the special ways (the ones in the IEP) to help Tyrone do well. Mr. White would still check in with him and talk with him about his behavior. It wasn't going to happen all at once. Tyrone would be able to try out the regular classroom in small steps.

Today, Tyrone is in regular classes full time. He still sees his counselor twice a week. He is even asked to talk to other kids who are getting ready to go back into regular ed. He tells them what it's like. He offers tips about things that will help them succeed there.

Yes, it can be scary to move into a regular classroom when you've been away so long. Like Tyrone, you might worry that kids will tease you. You might think that the teachers won't understand the best ways to help. Sometimes these things can happen. But not too often. And if you are ready to be in regular ed, you are ready to deal with problems that sometimes happen. You've been practicing!

"Mrs. Erdahl tries to help me do better in the regular class. We talk and practice things. She has a favorite saying: 'A ship is safe in the harbor, but that's not what ships are for.' She is helping me leave her special ed harbor and sail to regular ed." —Gina, 10

8 Tips for Feeling More at Ease in a Regular Class

1. Ask to meet your new teacher before you start the class.
2. Whenever you see the new teacher, say hi in a friendly way.
3. Say hi to the other kids in the class. Especially be sure to do this to the nice kids, the shy kids, and those who sit near you.
4. Ask for help when you need it, but try to do the work first.
5. Say thank you to the teacher when you leave the regular class each day.
6. Keep in touch with your special education teacher. Make a plan together for how you can do this.

> 7. Expect a few "bumps in the road." Maybe at first you will feel uncomfortable or have trouble getting along in the regular class. If this happens, talk to the regular teacher, your counselor, or your special education teacher.
>
> 8. Give the regular class your best try for at least two weeks. That will help you tell if you are ready to be in a regular class yet or not.

Once you have learned ways to be a success in school, it is time to try them in the regular class. The IEP team knows that you are ready to be there. Your new teachers have been told about the ways that help you learn and make good choices. And there's one really great thing about moving into a regular class: With so many more kids, you have more chances to make new friends.

> REMEMBER...
>
> **Sometimes all the "official" stuff can seem like a big hassle—labels, special classes,**

IEPs, goals to work on. You have to deal with different people and work on tough changes. These are the challenges you face. There was once a time when kids with BD couldn't get good help at school. But now, you get the support you need in order to succeed in school. Be patient with yourself and other people. Believe in yourself and don't give up! You CAN make the changes that will help you reach your goals.

And Now…

You've read about many ideas in this book. You've discovered lots of skills, tips, and information that you can use to succeed in meeting your challenge of making better behavior choices. The challenge for you *right now* is to choose some ideas that you read and actually try them. Then come back and try a few more ideas. Keep trying out new ways to make better choices. You'll find that you're learning more, making new and better friends, and getting along better with your teachers and family. You really, truly will.

Thanks for reading this book. You've learned a lot. You've probably already started to make some changes. Keep making those important changes. And keep believing in yourself!

While I was writing this book, a student told me: "My teachers keep telling me I can do anything if I work hard enough. I like that they believe in me." **I believe in YOU.**

Why would I believe in you when I haven't even met you? Because you're reading this book. The fact that you picked it up and read it means you are motivated and serious about making your life better. You have made a very smart choice by reading through this book. I know that you will make more great behavior choices because of what you read about, and because of what the trustworthy adults in school and at home are teaching you. If you took the time to read this book and think about the ideas inside, you have what it takes to be a winner in your behavior challenge!

I'm really interested in your struggles, your successes, and your progress. I would like to hear from you about how you're making smarter choices. If you would like to share, write to me at help4kids@freespirit.com . I'll write back.

Dr. Mac

Glossary

This part of the book explains the words that were shown in **black, bold** type in each chapter.

ADHD (attention deficit hyperactivity disorder): This label is given to kids who have lots of trouble sitting still and paying attention. Doctors sometimes prescribe medicine for kids with ADHD. The medicine helps these kids slow down and concentrate better.

anger management: Being able to control angry feelings is important. Counselors and teachers sometimes meet with groups of students who need to learn and practice ways to handle anger better. Counselors or psychologists might also work with individual students on these ways to stay in control. There are many books with lessons and activities that adults can use to teach kids how to manage their anger better. Section entitled "What About Resources for Grown-Ups?" tells where adults can find a list of some of these books.

assertive: People who are assertive speak up, in a strong but polite way. You are assertive if you say what's important to you *and* treat the other person with respect.

authority figure: This is an adult who is in charge of keeping kids safe and helping them make good choices. Teachers, principals, counselors, parents, guardians, and police officers are examples of authority figures.

BD (behavior disorder or behavior disordered): This is one of the labels given to kids whose behavior keeps teachers from teaching and keeps other kids and themselves from learning. Kids who need to learn to follow school rules or the directions of teachers might have this label. Different schools use different labels to identify kids who need a lot of help to make good behavior choices. Depending on the school, there may be different labels for BD. Some common ones are ED, EBD, or something different that really means the same thing.

behavior challenges: Kids who have behavior challenges are making some mistakes in their behavior choices.

Adults and other kids are getting worried about the behavior of these kids because they're getting in trouble more and more. These kids have the chance to make important changes before the school gives them the label of BD (see the previous term).

behavior modification (behavior mod): This is a scientific way of changing the behavior of people. When teachers or parents reward you for good behavior, they're using behavior mod. They're helping you change (modify) your behavior.

BIP (behavior intervention plan): This is a part of the IEP (individualized education program) that tells teachers the positive things they should do to help students with BD make better choices.

challenge: A challenge is something hard to do but worth working hard to achieve or overcome. When you are challenged, it means that you have to work hard to accomplish something.

conflict resolution: When kids are angry with each other, it's important for them to figure out how to solve their problem without getting violent.

Counselors and teachers sometimes meet with groups of students who need to learn and practice ways to solve problems together. There are books with lessons and activities that adults can use to teach kids how to resolve conflicts in helpful ways. Section entitled "What About Resources for Grown-Ups?" tells where adults can find a list of some of these books.

consultant teacher: This is a teacher who is trained to help kids with BD. Consultant teachers travel from school to school. They work with kids and also help teachers learn better ways to work with students who have BD.

counseling: This is a kind of help from a specially trained adult called a *counselor.* Counselors are trained to help kids understand their problems and challenges better. They also help kids figure out what to do about those problems.

criticize: To criticize means to tell someone that she or he isn't doing something right. When a person judges what another person does in this way, it's called *criticism.*

depression: Depression means feeling really sad most of the time. A person who is *depressed* feels sad, down, or bummed out most or all of the time. (Being sad sometimes or even for a few days is usually not the same as being depressed.)

EBD (emotional or behavioral disorder): This is one of the labels given to kids whose behavior keeps teachers from teaching and keeps other kids and themselves from learning. Kids who need to learn to follow school rules or the directions of teachers might have this label. Different schools use different labels. So some kids with similar problems might be labeled BD, ED, or something else.

ED (emotional disturbance): This is one of the labels given to kids whose behavior keeps teachers from teaching and keeps other kids and themselves from learning. Kids who need to learn to follow school rules or the directions of teachers might have this label. Different schools use different labels. So some kids with similar problems might be labeled BD, EBD, or something else.

FBA (functional behavior assessment): This is a way that adults figure out why a student sometimes makes wrong choices and misbehaves. The FBA helps adults at school decide what ways to help a student improve his or her ways of behaving. The FBA also helps the IEP team make a BIP (behavior intervention plan).

frustrated: When you're frustrated, you feel upset. You might get frustrated when people or things get in the way of something you want to do. *Frustration* happens when someone or something keeps you from reaching a goal that you want to achieve. Some people feel like they're going to burst. Good choices have to be made to keep frustration from turning into anger.

IDEA (Individuals with Disabilities Education Act): IDEA is the "special ed law" in the United States. It says that schools must do the right things for students with disabilities. With this law, the word "disabilities" includes kids with behavior disorders. IDEA says that schools must give these students the help they need to make better choices in school. Many other countries have laws similar to IDEA.

IEP (individualized education program): All students who have disabilities have their own IEPs in their school records. Kids labeled with a behavior disorder are included in this group. The IEP is a plan that tells how a student is doing in school, what she or he will learn during the school year, and how teachers will help the student reach goals. For kids with BD, the IEP also has a part called the BIP (behavior intervention plan). The BIP tells which behaviors they need to work on. The BIP also tells teachers positive ways to teach the new behaviors.

IEP team: This is a group of adults that decides if a student needs special education to learn and behave better in school. They also think of the ways to help students learn and behave better.

inclusion: Inclusion means having students with all kinds of special education needs in the regular classroom. Different kids are included for different amounts of time and different subjects. As students improve in making good choices, they are included in the regular classroom for more of the school day.

LD (learning difference, learning disability): This is a label given to kids who don't always learn as easily or in the same way as most of the other students. Kids with LD may need special help with some kinds of learning.

mentor: A mentor is a wise person who knows how to make good choices. It's a person who teaches others how to make good choices, too.

negative: This means not-so-nice or bad. "No" is a negative word. Wrong behavior is negative behavior. The opposite of negative is *positive,* which means good or nice.

paraprofessional: This is a person who is trained to help teachers do their jobs. Different paraprofessionals have different jobs and duties. Sometimes they work with kids who have BD in the regular or special classroom.

PBIS (positive behavioral interventions and supports): For kids with BD, there is a part of the individualized education program (IEP) called the behavior intervention plan (BIP). The BIP lists the positive ways that teachers are supposed to use to help BD students make better choices and behave better. These ways are called PBIS.

peer mediation: Some schools train kids to help other kids end their battles. This formal system in which kids help other kids solve problems is called peer mediation. *Peers* are people from the same age group or place. At school, you and the other students are peers. A peer mediator is a student who is trained to help both sides listen to each other and find a way to end the argument.

persistent: Being persistent means continuing to work at something that is hard to do. When you keep trying your best and working hard, you *persist*.

positive: This means nice or good. "Yes" is a positive word. Good behavior is positive behavior. The opposite of positive is *negative,* which means not-so-nice or bad.

potential: Potential means the possibility for doing well. Your potential is what you can be and what you can do if you work hard to make good decisions.

psychologist: A psychologist is trained to study the mind and how it works. Psychologists know how to find out what's bothering kids. They ask questions about feelings and what is happening. They have kids do things that will help discover what the problem is. Then the psychologists (and others) help kids solve the problems.

revenge: Revenge means doing something mean to someone because you think that person did something mean to you. Some kids want revenge when they get mad at someone. They try to hurt the other person or make him or her feel bad, too. Revenge makes things worse between people, not better.

schizophrenia: This is a disease that causes mixed-up chemicals in the brain. Kids with schizophrenia sometimes seem confused or show unusual behaviors. Medications help them see and understand the world better.

self-contained classroom: This is a classroom where kids in special education go to school for all (or most) of the day. Sometimes a self-contained class is called a "special class." Students with BD might be in a self-contained classroom all, most, or some of the time. Often they go to a regular education classroom for one or two subjects. If they do well in those classes, they will get a chance to go into a regular classroom more of the time.

self-esteem: Self-esteem is how you feel about yourself. People who like themselves have *high self-esteem.* People who don't feel good about themselves have *low self-esteem.* Teachers and counselors have ways to help kids improve their self-esteem.

self-talk: The things you think and say silently to yourself are self-talk. When people think to themselves about ways to stay calm, keep out of trouble, and make good decisions, they are using *positive self-talk.* They are telling themselves smart ways to handle a difficult situation.

shaping: With shaping, you build a good behavior in steps. You set small goals to get you to a big behavior goal. Each time you meet a small goal, you set another small goal. Each small goal gets you closer to the bigger behavior goal. The small goals lead you to reaching the big goal that you want to accomplish.

shaping plan: This is a kind of plan you write down. You write your big goal and how you're doing with that goal now. Then, in between now and reaching your big goal, you write the small goals in the order that you will work on them to meet your larger goal.

social skills: These are skills people need to get along with other people. Someone with good social skills gets along well with others. Kids with poor social skills have trouble making friends. They also have problems doing the right thing when they are talking or working with others. Some schools hold special classes or groups where students learn social skills. There are books with lessons and activities that adults can use to teach these skills. Section entitled "What About Resources for Grown-Ups?" tells where adults can find a list of some of these books.

special classroom: This is a classroom where kids in special education go to school for all (or most) of the day. Sometimes a special class is called a "self-contained class." Students with BD might be in a self-contained classroom all, most, or some of the time. Often they go to a regular education classroom for one or two subjects. If they do well in those classes, they will get a chance to go into a regular classroom more of the time.

special education (special ed): This is the term for the special services, supports, and other kinds of help that schools give to students with special needs. These students may have behavior challenges, learning differences, or physical disabilities.

special needs: These are needs that can be met best in special education. Kids with BD have special needs. They need to learn to choose better behavior and actions so they can learn and get along in school.

stress: Stress is the pressure or tension you feel sometimes in your mind or body. When you feel tense or upset, you are under stress.

support group: This is a group that meets with a counselor or another specially trained adult to talk about a problem or challenge. Some kids with BD meet in a support group with a counselor. They talk about their behavior problems and how they're doing when it comes to making better choices.

survive: This means to keep going and become stronger when things are difficult. *Survival* skills (like the ones you learn in this book) can help you keep going and succeed. They can help you get along with teachers, other kids, and adults at home even though you have behavior challenges.

Solutions to Some of the Challenges and Questions

Sam's Smart Choices

2. Sam's words tell the boys that he knows about insulting mothers. He also shows that he is too mature (grown up) and cool to get involved in the "game."
4. Sam thinks his mom is great. He realizes that this is what's important. His self-talk helps him avoid having to defend his mom. He doesn't get trapped in a war of words. He remembers to stop and think before choosing what to say.
5. Sam has hurt feelings, but he stops, thinks, and chooses. He controls himself. That is a very mature response. He sees that if he falls into the boys' trap, the insults will continue or get worse.
7. Sam chooses a good way to handle his feelings. He shares his problem with a friend to feel better. Someday he'll be there to listen when his friend has a problem.

8. Sam defends his mom and then leaves. He doesn't want to show the behavior that makes trouble for him. His ready reply lets him stand up for his mom without getting into a conversation that sometimes leads to a fight.

Sam's Poor Choices

1. Sam does what the boys want him to do: He gets into a war of words. It's a war he probably can't win. What happens? He acts like the kids who are making him feel bad. He says things that he hates to hear. That doesn't make sense.
3. Sam shows the others that the insults upset him. Now the boys will say those insults again. Sam will probably get sent to the principal, too. He'll probably be punished for hitting others.

What About Choice 6?

It's hard to know how this choice will work. It could be a strong, friendly response. It could also seem bossy. It depends on how Sam says the words

and how he looks when he speaks. *How you say and do things can be just as important as the words you use.*
1. B
2. C (choice 2 is an assertive response)
3. A

These answers show one way to change the you-talk to I-talk. There are lots of ways to do this, so your answers might be different. That's okay. Just be sure NOT to use the word "you" to tell people they are wrong.

CHALLENGE 1

"Mrs. Travis, I've tried again. I guess I just forgot what to do. Could I please have help on one problem so I can remember what to do on the rest of them?"

CHALLENGE 2

When Maggie sees that her watch is gone, she can say: "My watch is missing. Did anyone borrow it?"

If no one says anything, Maggie can go quietly to the teacher and say: "Mr. Tess, my watch was on my desk and now it's gone. Could you please help me find out if someone took it?"

CHALLENGE 3

"Sasha, weren't we supposed to start by writing about the answers that are wrong? And tell why they're wrong? I've got the dates and places we needed for the beginning of the paper. How can we get them in there?"

CHALLENGE 4

Ira can speak for the other kids if they agree. He can talk to Mr. C. as he enters class instead of at science time: "Hey, Mr. C. We talked about the way we acted earlier today, and we were wrong. But we were really looking forward to the trip. Is there anything we can do to earn back the trip?"

CHALLENGE 1

In this sandwich, the request (the middle of the sandwich) is highlighted in *italics:*

"Miss Lange, I agree with you that it is important to do my schoolwork.

But I think a zero grade is unfair. I couldn't do the paper last night because I left my notebook at Paula's. *Could I please turn it in after lunch?* That's when I'll see her and get my notebook back. I really enjoyed doing the report on Ben Franklin, and learned a lot. I think you'll like the paper if you take it late."

CHALLENGE 2

There are lots of ways Aron could make his request sandwich. Yours will probably be different from the one here. That's okay. Just be sure to start and end with something nice. Remember to make your request firm and friendly. In this sandwich, the request (the middle of the sandwich) is highlighted in *italics:*

"Mr. Hunter, I don't want to miss the explanation. I really like doing your projects, and I don't want to miss the instructions. *Could I please have another chance and stay here now?* Next time I'll know I'm supposed to be in my seat, not just in the room. I'm glad you explained that to me."

- Nina remembered her goal.

- She used "Stop, Think, Choose, and Think Again."
- She showed respect.
- When she spoke, she used assertive I-talk.
- She made a request sandwich.

CHALLENGE 1

1. Compliment sandwich
2. Complaint
3. Request sandwich

CHALLENGE 2

Here is one possible compliment sandwich. The compliment (the middle of the sandwich) is highlighted in *italics:*

"I don't want anyone doing this puzzle without asking me. Please ask first *like you do before coming in my side of the room. It's been great since you started doing that.* So please ask me before you work on my puzzle."

Here is one possible request sandwich. The request (the middle of the sandwich) is highlighted in *italics:*

"It's nice that you want to help with the puzzle. I want to keep the part that's already done, though. Otherwise the pieces get messed up. *I need you to ask me if you want to do this puzzle.* You do a good job of asking before you go in my part of the bedroom, so I know you can do a good job about the puzzle, too. Thanks."

Here's Dr. Mac's list of things that tell you when you've made a smart choice:

- You stay out of trouble in school and get along better with teachers.
- You learn more in school because you're listening and paying attention.
- You hear people say nice things about you.
- You make more friends—the good kind.
- You become a better friend.
- You stay out of trouble with the police and other adults.
- You feel happier at home.
- You get along better with people in your family.
- You feel better about yourself.
- Your future looks brighter.

And **SOMEDAY,** when you get really good at making smart choices…
- **You won't be labeled BD anymore.**

303

What other ones did you think of?

Resources for You

Books

Look for these books at the library or bookstore. If a book isn't on the shelf, the librarian or store clerk can find or order a copy. You can also visit libraries and bookstores on the Internet.

The ADHD Workbook for Kids by Lawrence E. Shapiro (Oakland, CA: Instant Help Books, 2010). This workbook gives you practical ways to handle ADHD, control your behavior, and get along better at school and at home.

Basic Social Skills for Youth: A Handbook from Boys Town by Father Flanagan's Boys' Home (Boys Town, NE: Boys Town Press, 2007). This small book covers eight social skills that are really important for you to know. Find out why it's important to follow instructions, show respect, and notice the feelings of others.

Bystander Power: Now with Anti-Bullying Action by Phyllis Kaufman Goodstein and Elizabeth Verdick

(Minneapolis: Free Spirit Publishing, 2012). This book shows how important bystanders—the people who see bullying or know about it, but don't do anything—are in stopping bullying or allowing it to continue.

Dude, That's Rude! (Get Some Manners) by Pamela Espeland and Elizabeth Verdick (Minneapolis: Free Spirit Publishing, 2007). If your behavior challenges ever show up as bad manners, this book will help you with Power Words to use and P.U. Words to avoid, the essentials of e-tiquette (politeness online), and more.

Help! My Teacher Hates Me by Meg Schneider (New York: Workman Publishing, 1994). Find out how to get along better with teachers and other adults at school. Also learn ways to improve your grades and solve lots of school problems.

How to Handle Bullies, Teasers, and Other Meanies by Kate Cohen-Posey (Highland City, FL: Rainbow Books, 1995). This book is about teasing, name-calling, prejudice, anger, and conflict. It gives lots of positive ways to deal with difficult situations.

How to Take the GRRRR Out of Anger by Elizabeth Verdick and Marjorie Lisovskis (Minneapolis: Free Spirit Publishing, 2003). Everybody feels angry at times. The key is learning how to manage anger. This book uses humor and teaches tricks and skills that can help.

Kids' Random Acts of Kindness by the editors of Conari Press (Berkeley: Conari Press, 1994). Read real stories from kids who have done kind, helpful things. Learn how you can make a difference in your school and community, too.

Let's Be Friends by Lawrence E. Shapiro and Julia Holmes (Oakland, CA: Instant Help Books, 2008). This workbook suggests lots of ways to make connections and build friendships.

Siblings: You're Stuck with Each Other, So Stick Together by James J. Crist and Elizabeth Verdick (Minneapolis: Free Spirit Publishing, 2010). Brothers and sisters: they can make great friends, and it's nice to have someone who'll love you no matter what. But siblings can be a real drag, too. With this book, learn how to get along better and how to cope with problems of fairness, jealousy, conflict, tattling, and privacy.

Stick Up for Yourself! Every Kid's Guide to Personal Power and Positive Self-Esteem by Gershen Kaufman, Lev Raphael, and Pamela Espeland (Minneapolis: Free Spirit Publishing, 1999). This is a book with lots of great tips on how to be assertive. It can help you feel good about yourself and be firm and polite with others.

Too Old for This, Too Young for That! Your Survival Guide for the Middle-School Years by Harriet S. Mosatche and Karen Unger (Minneapolis: Free Spirit Publishing, 2010). Middle school brings lots of changes. School gets harder. Home life and friendships sometimes do, too. This book offers tips just for middle-school kids. Find ways to set goals, make good choices, and take charge of your life.

What Do You Really Want? How to Set a Goal and Go for It! by Beverly K. Bachel (Minneapolis: Free Spirit Publishing, 2001). Setting goals can help you succeed in school, ease stress, and boost your self-esteem. This book is a step-by-step guide that makes setting goals easy and fun.

What to Do When You Grumble Too Much by Dawn Huebner (Washington, DC: Magination Press, 2006). This book is full of simple ideas for staying positive and not letting frustration and other negative feelings drag you down. Also check out *What to Do When Your Temper Flares* (a book about controlling anger) and *What to Do When Bad Habits Take Hold* (about breaking troublesome habits and building smarter ones).

Websites

Check out these websites for tips, tactics, and ideas about making smart choices and dealing with difficult situations. (And always remember to check in with an adult before using the Internet.)

Kidscape (www.kidscape.org.uk). This website offers a lot of great advice for dealing with bullies. Also find tips for making friends and getting along with difficult people.

KidsHealth (www.kidshealth.org/kid). This site offers lots of information on different issues facing kids today. You'll find ways to handle feelings, get along with others, deal with tough situations, and stay healthy and safe. You can also learn where to turn for more help if you need it.

McGruff the Crime Dog (www.McGruff.org). This site features games, videos, and advice about handling different kinds of bullying.

PBS Kids (www.PBSKids.org). This site teaches information in interesting ways. It also shows kids making good decisions.

Organizations

These are all national organizations. You can visit their websites, write, or call for more information. (Phone numbers beginning with "800" are free to call. The others may cost money. Check with an adult before calling the numbers that are not free.) You can also look in the phone book for a club or group near you.

Big Brothers Big Sisters of America • 230 North 13th Street • Philadelphia, PA 19107 • www.bbbs.org

Sometimes having an adult friend can make all the difference as you try to improve your behavior. This organization arranges adult mentors for kids. On the website, click on "Enroll a Child" to find out how to contact a group near you.

Boys and Girls Clubs of America • 1275 Peachtree Street NE • Atlanta, GA 30309 • (404) 487-5700 • www.bgca.org

Want to become friends with other kids and adults in your neighborhood? These clubs have all kinds of activities that are both fun and educational. If you're looking for a little support as you try to be your best, this is a great resource for you.

Boy Scouts of America • P.O. Box 152079 • Irving, TX 75015 • (972) 580-2000 • www.scouting.org

Scouting is a great way to try new things, learn to make good decisions, and make friends. It's fun, too.

Girl Scouts of the USA • 420 Fifth Avenue • New York, NY 10018 • 1-800-478-7248 • www.girlscouts.org

In Girl Scouts, you can build skills for succeeding in school and at home while enjoying fun activities and events.

YMCA of the USA • 101 North Wacker Drive • Chicago, IL 60606 • 1-800-872-9622 • www.ymca.net

The "Y" has gyms and sports activities. It has fun learning activities and day camps, too. You can join a class, go swimming, or play sports. The YMCA is for boys and girls.

What About Resources for Grown-Ups?

Teachers and parents want to help you learn to behave better and make good choices. There are lots of books and lessons that can help them understand the best ways to do this. I have made a list of these resources. Tell the adults in your life about this list. They can find it on my publisher's website at www.freespirit.com/SG4K-behavior-forms. Use the password 4smartchoices.

Other Great Books from Free Spirit

The Survival Guide for Kids with ADHD
Updated Edition
by John F. Taylor, Ph.D.
This book helps kids with ADHD know that they're not alone and offers practical strategies for taking care of oneself, modifying behavior, enjoying school, having fun, and dealing with doctors, counselors, and medication. For ages 8–12.
128 pp.; softcover; 2-color; illust.; 6" x 9"

What to Do When You're Cranky & Blue: A Guide for Kids
by James J. Crist, Ph.D.
Kids can turn to this book for support, encouragement, and ideas for coping when they feel bad, sad, grumpy, or lonely. Kids discover lots of ideas they can use to talk about feelings, boost their self-esteem, make and keep friends, and enjoy their alone time. A special section addresses hard-to-handle feelings like depression and grief. For ages 9–13.
128 pp.; softcover; 2-color; illust.; $5^{3}/_{8}$" x $8^{3}/_{8}$"

How to Do Homework Without Throwing Up
written and illustrated by Trevor Romain
This book features hilarious cartoons and witty insights that teach important truths about homework and positive, practical strategies for getting it done. For ages 8–13.
72 pp.; softcover; illust.; $5^{1}/_{8}$" x 7"

Cliques, Phonies, & Other Baloney
written and illustrated by Trevor Romain
Sound advice and witty cartoons help kids deal with cliques and develop the skills they need to form positive, healthy relationships and build self-esteem. For ages 8–13.
136 pp.; softcover; illust.; $5^{1}/_{8}$" x 7"

Find all the Free Spirit **SURVIVAL GUIDES** for Kids
at www.freespirit.com/survival-guides-for-kids

Interested in purchasing multiple quantities and receiving volume discounts?
Contact edsales@freespirit.com or call 1.800.735.7323 and ask for Education Sales.

Many Free Spirit authors are available for speaking engagements, workshops, and keynotes. Contact speakers@freespirit.com or call 1.800.735.7323.

For pricing information, to place an order, or to request a free catalog, contact:
Free Spirit Publishing Inc.
217 Fifth Avenue North • Suite 200 • Minneapolis, MN 55401-1299 • toll-free 800.735.7323
local 612.338.2068 • fax 612.337.5050 • help4kids@freespirit.com • www.freespirit.com

Back Cover Material

- Is it hard for you to get along with teachers, family, and others?
- Do you wish you got in trouble less often?
- Do you have a tough time making good choices, even when you try hard?
- Are you ready to make a change for the better?

"Chock-full of information."

—*School Library Journal's Curriculum Connections* (praise for the previous edition)

If you answered **yes** to any of these questions, this book is for **you.** Like a lot of kids with behavior challenges, you know that they're no fun. And it's not easy to change habits and learn new ways. But **you can do it,** and this book can help. It's full of ideas for you to try. These ideas have worked for other kids with behavior challenges, and they can work for you.

***

What's Inside?

True stories about kids with behavior challenges • Smart choices for dealing with feelings • Ways to get along better at school and at home • Ideas for making and keeping good friends • A glossary of helpful words • A special section about behavior labels like BD and SED • **And much more!**

***

Tom McIntyre (Dr. Mac) is a professor of behavior disorders and special education at Hunter College of the City University of New York. He is a popular workshop presenter and keynote speaker.

Index

A

Acting without thinking, *16*
Actions,
    See Behavior,
Activities,
    after-school, *151, 153, 156*
Adults,
    at home,
        asking, for help, *170*
        talking to teachers, *189, 190*
        telling, about choices, *189*
        using point sheets with, *182, 183*
        using talking and listening skills with, *165, 168, 170*
    who don't understand, *161, 162, 165*
    kinds of caring, reactions from, *14*
    school as preparation for being, *206*
    trusted finding, *37, 39*
    practicing choices with, *65*
    talking to, *20, 34, 37, 136*
    working with, *4*
    See also Teachers,
After-school activities, *151, 153, 156*
Anger management,
    group in school, *55, 251*
    when want revenge, *251*

working with counselor on, *34*
Apologies, *213*
Appointments, keeping, *199*
Assertive, Assertiveness
  described, *76, 78*
  instead of becoming angry, *86*
  practicing, *85*
  wrong time for being, *121*
Attention, need for, *250*
Authority figures, dealing with, *74*

B

Bad choices,
  how to avoid, *47, 49*
  reasons for, *16*
  results of, *14, 56, 242*
  taking responsibility for, *211, 213*
  telling difference between smart and, *214*
BD (behavior disorder) label,
  feelings about having, *236, 237*
  getting extra help in school and, *229, 230, 233, 259, 261*
  law requiring, *257, 259*
  meaning of, *229, 230, 233*
  other names for, *227*
  reaction of others to, *235, 236*
  reasons for,
    brain chemical mix ups, *246, 263, 265*
    low self-esteem, *253, 255*
    making bad choices, *242*
    misbehaving to get attention, *250*

poor anger management skills, *251*
using as excuse, *237, 239*
what it does not mean, *230, 233, 235*
Beat Your Previous Best form, *99, 101, 110*
Behavior,
   ignoring mean, *37, 72, 74*
   keeping track of, *96, 99*
   rewarding wanted, *131, 133, 134*
   shaping positive, *101, 103, 104, 112*
Behavior challenges,
   gripes of kids with,
Behavior mod or modification,
   using, *131, 133, 134*
BIP (behavior intervention plan),
   described, *263*
   as part of IEP, *259*

Blaming statements, *83*
Brain chemical mix ups, *246*
Bravery, your, *9*

C

Calendar, listing daily help you gave, *32*
Career ideas, *216, 218*
Change,
   having patience and persistence for, *9, 213, 219, 221, 270*
   having potential for, *255*
   setting goals for, *101, 103, 104*
   starting point of, *4, 7, 9*
   using behavior mod to, *131, 133, 134*
Choices,
   making,
      getting help with,
      thinking about previous, *39*

taking responsibility for, *211, 213, 223, 224*
  See also Bad choices; Smart choices,
Class rules, *90, 92*
Comments,
  making 'sandwich' with, *126, 128, 129, 131*
  phrasing as questions, *121, 124*
Compliments,
  giving, *117, 119, 143*
  phrasing comments as, *126, 128, 129, 131*
  sandwiches, *171, 172, 174*
Conflict resolution, *251*
Contracts with teachers, *107, 109, 113*
Control, making bad choices and losing, *16*
Counselors,
  talking about teachers with, *136*
  working with school, *34, 37*
Crisis intervention, finding, *20*

D

Deep breathing, *39, 42*
Difficult people, dealing with,
  ignoring mean words and actions, *37, 72, 74*
  practicing, *79, 83, 85*
  using I-talk, *81*
  See also Smart choices,

E

Eating right, *199*
EBD (emotional or behavioral disorder) label,
  See also BD (behavior disorder) label,
ED (emotional disturbance) label,

See also BD (behavior disorder) label,
Exercise,
  for breaking habits, *101*
  importance of, *20*
  making smart choices and, *42*
Experiences,
  learning from, *214*
  writing down,
Expert, becoming, *145, 150*

F

Family adults, See Adults,
FBA (functional behavior assessment), *263*
Feelings,
  about class placement, *270*
  about having BD label, *236, 237*
  acting on, *18*
  drawing pictures about, *39*
  having upset, *14*
  managing anger, *55, 251*
  talking about, *34, 37, 39*
  writing about, *20*
Foster parents, See Adults
Friends,
  making,
    by asking questions, *145*
    by giving compliments, *143*
    by helping, *145, 150, 151*
  places to find, *145*
  qualities of good, *158*
  talking to, *37*
  warning signals from, *94*
Future,
  preparing for, *206, 208, 211, 213, 214*
  thinking about careers, *216, 218*

G

Goal record, keeping, *96, 99, 109*
Goals, setting, *101, 103, 104*
Golden rule, *208*
Greeting teachers, *116, 119*
Gripes, common,
Grown-ups,
  See Adults,
Guardians,
  See Adults,

H

Habits, exercise for breaking, *101*
Help,
  getting,
    at home, *170*
    right away, *20*
    in school and BD label,
  offering,
    at home, *201*
    making friends and, *145, 150, 151*
  as part of being friend, *158*
  unwanted, *196*
Helping habits, *30, 32*
Hobbies, *201*
Home life,
  adults in,
    asking for help, *170*
    talking to teachers, *189, 190*
    telling, about choices, *189*
    using point sheets with, *182, 183*
    using talking and listening skills with, *165, 168, 170*
    who don't understand, *161, 162, 165*
  building self-esteem, *202*
  causes of arguments, *193*
  doing kind things, *196*
  eating right, *199*
  hobbies, *201*

keeping appointments, *199*
making plan to solve problems, *190, 193*
relaxing, *201*
saying thank you, *196, 199*
taking medicines, *199*
taking time-outs, *176, 182*

I

I Can sign, *221*
IDEA (Individuals with Disabilities Education Act) law, *257, 259*
Ideas, writing down,
IEP (individualized education program),
  having questions about, *267*
  parts of, *259, 261, 263*
IEP team,
  FBA assessment by, *263*
  job of, *261*
  meetings of, *263*
Inclusion,
  described, *267*
  feelings about, *270*
  not wanting, *272, 274*
  tips for successful, *276*
  ways of, *265, 267*
I-talk,
  described, *81, 85, 86*
  using at home, *168*
  using in journal, *83*
  using in school, *121*

J

Journals,
  calendar with daily help you gave, *32*
  job ideas, *216*
  keeping,

list of possible adults to talk to, *37*
using I-talk, *83*
writing about feelings in, *20, 39*
writing replies in, *63, 65*

K
Kindness, at home, *196*

L
Listening skills, using, *165, 168, 170*
Loyalty, *158*

M
Mean words, dealing with,
  being assertive, *76, 78, 85, 86*
  ignoring, *37, 72, 74*
Medicines, taking, *199, 246, 265*
Mentors, *150*
Mirror talking, *28, 63*
Mistakes, admitting, *213*

N
National Youth Crisis Hotline, *20*
Negative friendships, *158, 159*
Negative thoughts, making bad choices and, *16*
Notebooks,
  See Journals,

P
Paraprofessionals, *265*
Parents,
  See Adults,
Patience, importance of, *213*
PBIS (Positive Behavioral Intervention and Supports), *263*
Peer mediation, *251*
Persistence,
  importance of, *213*
Pictures, drawing about feelings, *39*
Plus (+) and minus (-) record, *99*

Point sheets, *182, 183*
Practice,
  apologizing, *213*
  being assertive, *85*
  dealing with difficult people, *79, 83, 85*
  handling situations effectively, *59*
  I-talking, *85, 86*
  mirror talking, *28, 63*
  ready replies, *63*
  reasons for, *2*
  relaxing, *42*
  saying smart choices you made, *39*
  talking about goals, *170*
  telling difference between smart and bad choices, *214*
  thinking before acting, *65*
  using compliment sandwiches, *174*
  using request sandwiches, *129, 131, 174*
Pressure, responding to, *14*
Pride and progress exercises, *22, 24, 26*
Progress trackers, *96, 99, 109*

Q

Questions,
  asking, to make friends, *145*
  making suggestions with, *121, 123, 124*
  phrasing comments as, *126, 128, 129, 131*

R

Ready replies,
  planning forms for, *65, 66*
  using, *56*
Ready Ruler, marking, *4, 7, 9*
Regrets, having, *47*
Relaxation,

at home, *201*
importance of, *20*
making smart choices and, *39, 42*
practicing, *42*
Requests, making sandwich of, *126, 128, 129, 131, 172, 174*
Respect, *158*
Responsibility,
  form, *223, 224*
  taking, *211, 213*
Revenge, *251*
Rules in school, *90, 92*

S

Sandwiches,
  making compliment, *171, 172, 174*
  making request, *126, 128, 129, 131, 172, 174*
School,
  anger management group in, *55, 251*
  BD label and getting extra help in, *229, 230, 233, 259, 261*
  counselors, *34, 37*
  inclusion in regular education classes,
    not wanting, *272, 274*
    tips for successful, *276*
    ways of, *265, 267*
  law requiring BD program, *257, 259*
  making smart choices in,
    getting help from friends, *94*
    making contracts with teachers, *107, 109, 113*
    preparing for, *90, 92*
    putting skills together, *136, 138, 140*
    recording progress, *96, 99, 101, 109, 110*

participating in activities after, *151, 153, 156*
as preparation for being adult, *206*
rules, *90, 92*
self-contained classrooms, *267*
talking to adults in, *34, 37, 39, 136*
Score Points at Home sheets, *182, 183*
Self-contained classrooms, *267*
Self-esteem,
  building,
    helping habits for, *30, 32*
    at home, *202*
    pride and progress exercises for, *22, 24, 26*
    smart choices and, *20*
  reasons for low, *253, 255*
Self-talk,
  ignoring mean words and actions with, *37, 72, 74*
  using to avoid bad choices, *47, 49*
Shaping plan, *101, 103, 104, 112*
Sharing, *158*
Signals, preparing warning, *94*
Smart choices,
  making,
    contracts with teachers, *107, 109, 113*
    exercise and, *42*
    getting help from friends and, *94*
    preparing for, in school, *90, 92*
    relaxation and, *39, 42*
    working at, *242, 244*
  recording progress, *96, 99, 101, 109, 110*
  results of, *14, 56*

telling adults at home about, *189*
telling difference between bad and, *214*
Smartness, your, *9*
Social skills, lessons, *145, 244*
Solutions,
 thinking about, *61*
 using ready replies, *56*
Speaking up, *76, 78*
Special class or classroom,
 described, *267*
 feelings about, *270*
 IEP team and, *261*
Special education or special ed,
 being in, *235, 236, 237*
 IDEA law and, *257, 259*
Stepparents,
 See Adults,
Strength, your, *9*
Stress,
 from bad choices, *14*
 reducing with pride and progress exercises, *22, 24, 26*
 from returning to regular class, *272, 274*
Suggestions, making, *121, 123, 124*
Support groups, *251*

T

Talking skills,
 describing feelings, *34, 37, 39*
 I-talk,
  described, *81, 85, 86*
  using at home, *168*
  using in journal, *83*
  using in school, *121*
 using at home, *165, 168, 170*
Teachers,
 allowing, to teach, *119, 121*

complimenting, *117, 119*
greeting, *116, 119*
making contracts with, *107, 109, 113*
talking to adults at home, *189, 190*
talking to counselors about, *136*
using behavior mod with, *131, 133, 134*

Teasing, dealing with, *61, 63*
Thank you, saying, *196, 199*
Thinking,
  about solutions, *61*
  before acting, *47, 49, 65*
  negatively, *16*
Thoughts, writing down,
  See Journals,
Time-outs, *176, 182*

V
Volunteering help, *30, 32*

W
Warning signals, *94*
Words, ignoring mean, *37, 72, 74*
Writing,
  See Journals,

Y
You-talk, *81*

www.ingramcontent.com/pod-product-compliance
Lightning Source LLC
Chambersburg PA
CBHW052142300426
44115CB00011B/1490